EARLY CHILDH

M000312466

In the past several years, models of multi-tiered service delivery have emerged as a framework for supporting the needs of school-aged children in schools across the country and have received much attention in scholarly publications of education and related fields. Despite the needs of young children and the promise of early intervention, however, models of multi-tiered service delivery are only in the beginning stages of development in early childhood education settings such as preschools. This text provides early childhood professionals with an introduction to tiered service delivery and practical considerations in the implementation of a multi-tier system of supports with particular emphasis on early childhood law and ethics, assessment and intervention, developmental disabilities, and family engagement.

Gina Coffee, PhD, is a faculty member in the school psychology program at Loyola University Chicago and a nationally certified school psychologist. In practice, teaching, and research, Dr. Coffee focuses on the prevention of academic, behavioral, social, emotional, and health difficulties in children through collaboration with educators, parents, and community members. In 2010, she was awarded the Early Career Research Award by the Society for the Study of School Psychology.

Corey E. Ray-Subramanian, PhD, is a licensed psychologist who provides clinical services to children with developmental disabilities and their families through the Waisman Center at the University of Wisconsin-Madison. She is also involved in federally funded research related to children with autism spectrum disorders. Prior to her work at the Waisman Center, Dr. Ray-Subramanian was on the faculty in the department of psychology at Northern Illinois University.

G. Thomas Schanding, Jr., PhD, is a licensed psychologist, licensed specialist in school psychology, and nationally certified school psychologist working with Sheldon Independent School District in Houston, TX. He serves as the associate director of outreach/core faculty member in Special Education for the LoneStar LEND with the University of Texas Health Science Center and previously taught in the school psychology program at the University of Houston.

Kelly A. Feeney-Kettler, PhD, is an educational consultant in New Jersey. She earned a PhD in educational psychology, with a specialization in school psychology, from the University of Wisconsin-Madison and was recognized by Division 16 of the APA with an outstanding dissertation award. She held a postdoctoral fellowship with a concentration in early childhood at Vanderbilt University and received the Early Career Scholar Award from the Society for the Study of School Psychology.

Routledge
Taylor & Francis Group

School-Based Practice in Action Series
Series Editors
Rosemary B. Mennuti, EdD, NCSP
and
Ray W. Christner, PsyD, NCSP
Cognitive Health Solutions, LLC

This series provides school-based practitioners with concise practical guidebooks that are designed to facilitate the implementation of evidence-based programs into school settings, putting the best practices *in action*.

Assessment and Intervention for Executive Function Difficulties
George McCloskey, Lisa A. Perkins, and Bob Van Divner

Resilient Playgrounds
Beth Doll

Comprehensive Planning for Safe Learning Environments: A School Counselor's Guide to Integrating Physical and Psychological Safety - Prevention through Recovery
Melissa A. Reeves, Linda M. Kanan, Amy E. Plog

Behavioral Interventions in Schools: A Response-to-Intervention Guidebook
David M. Hulac, Joy Terrell, Odell Vining, and Joshua Bernstein

The Power of Family-School Partnering (FSP): A Practical Guide for School Mental Health Professionals and Educators
Cathy Lines, Gloria Miller, and Amanda Arthur-Stanley

Implementing Response-to-Intervention in Elementary and Secondary Schools: Procedures to Assure Scientific-Based Practices, Second Edition
Matthew K. Burns and Kimberly Gibbons

A Guide to Psychiatric Services in Schools: Understanding Roles, Treatment, and Collaboration
Shawna S. Brent

Comprehensive Children's Mental Health Services in Schools and Communities
Robyn S. Hess, Rick Jay Short, and Cynthia Hazel

Responsive School Practices to Support Lesbian, Gay, Bisexual, Transgender, and Questioning Students and Families
Emily Fisher and Kelly Kennedy

Pediatric School Psychology: Conceptualization, Applications, and Leadership Development
Thomas J. Power and Kathy L. Bradley-Klug

Serving the Gifted: Evidence-Based Clinical and Psychoeducational Practice
Steven I. Pfeiffer

Early Childhood Education: A Practical Guide to Evidence-Based, Multi-Tiered Service Delivery
Gina Coffee, Corey E. Ray-Subramanian, G. Thomas Schanding, Jr., and Kelly A. Feeney-Kettler

Implementing Response-to-Intervention to Address the Needs of English-Language Learners: Instructional Strategies and Assessment Tools for School Psychologists
Holly S. Hudspath-Niemi and Mary Lou Conroy

Conducting Student-Driven Interviews: Practical Strategies for Increasing Student Involvement and Addressing Behavior Problems
John Murphy

EARLY CHILDHOOD EDUCATION

A Practical Guide to Evidence-Based, Multi-Tiered Service Delivery

Gina Coffee,

Corey E. Ray-Subramanian,

G. Thomas Schanding, Jr.,

and Kelly A. Feeney-Kettler

 Routledge

Taylor & Francis Group

NEW YORK AND LONDON

First published 2013
by Routledge
711 Third Avenue, New York, NY 10017

Simultaneously published in the UK
by Routledge
27 Church Road, Hove, East Sussex BN3 2FA

Library of Congress Cataloging in Publication Data
Coffee, Gina.
    Early childhood education : a practical guide to evidence-based, multi-tiered service delivery / Gina Coffee, Corey E. Ray-Subramanian, G. Thomas Schanding and Kelly A. Feeney-Kettler.
    ISBN 978-0-415-50646-5 (hardback) — ISBN 978-0-415-50647-2 (paperback) — ISBN 978-0-203-12687-5 (e-book) (print)
    1. Early childhood special education. 2. Early childhood education—Curricula. 3. Early childhood education—Moral and ethical aspects. 4. Children with disabilities—Education. I. Title.
    LC4801.5.C64 2013
    372.21—dc23
    2012031609

ISBN: 978-0-415-50646-5 (hbk)
ISBN: 978-0-415-50647-2 (pbk)
ISBN: 978-0-203-12687-5 (ebk)

Typeset in Garamond
by EvS Communication Networx, Inc.

SUSTAINABLE
FORESTRY
INITIATIVE

Certified Sourcing
www.sfiprogram.org
SFI-00555
The SFI label applies to the text stock.

Printed and bound in the United States of America by
Walsworth Publishing Company, Marceline, MO.

Contents

Series Editors' Foreword   vii

Chapter 1   An Introduction to Evidence-Based Early Childhood
            Education Practice Within a Multitiered Service Delivery
            Model   1

Chapter 2   The Law, Ethical Standards, and Guidelines for MTSS in
            Early Childhood Education   10

Chapter 3   Universal Screening of Early Academic Skills   20

Chapter 4   Academic Interventions and Progress Monitoring: Tiers
            1, 2, and 3   33

Chapter 5   Universal Screening of Social-Emotional and Behavioral
            Functioning   45

Chapter 6   Social-Emotional and Behavioral Interventions and
            Progress Monitoring: Tiers 1, 2, and 3   61

Chapter 7   Developmental Disability Identification and
            Considerations for Inclusion   75

Chapter 8   Family Engagement in Early Childhood Education   91

Chapter 9   Summary and Future Directions for Early Childhood
            MTSS   105

References   111
Index   119

Series Editors' Foreword

We are delighted to see the continued growth of the *School-Based Practice in Action* series, which grew out of a discussion between us several years ago while attending a professional conference. At that time, we were each at different points in our careers, yet we both realized and faced the same challenges for educating and serving children and families. Acknowledging the transformations facing the educational system, we shared a passion and vision in ensuring quality services to schools, students, and families. This vision involved increasing the strong knowledge base of practitioners together with an impact on service delivery. This would require understanding theory and research, and most critically, providing resources to bridge empirical knowledge and the process of practice. Thus, our goal for the *School-Based Practice in Action* series has been to offer resources for readers based on sound research and principles that can be set directly "into action."

To accomplish this, each book in the series offers information in a practice-friendly manner, and each offers a web-link to obtain reproducible and usable materials that supplement the content of the book. These resources are designed to have a direct impact on transitioning research and knowledge into the day-to-day functions of school-based practitioners. We recognize that the implementation of programs and the changing of roles come with challenges and barriers, and as such, these may take on various forms depending on the context of the situation and the voice of the practitioner. To that end, the books of the *School-Based Practice in Action* series may be used in their entirety and present form for a number of practitioners; however, for others, these books will help them find new ways to move toward effective action and new possibilities. No matter which style fits your practice, we hope that these books will influence your work and professional growth.

We are grateful to have had the opportunity to work with Drs. Coffee, Ray-Subramanian, Schanding, and Feeney-Kettler in the development of this book, *Early Childhood Education: A Practical Guide to Evidence-Based,*

Multitiered Service Delivery. Since the inception of this series, we have wanted to publish a book on working with young children to enhance academic and social–emotional functioning. However, we felt that it was essential that the book for this series offer information on early childhood education that is aligned with current trends and research in education. Our wait to find the right authors was worth it, as Coffee, Ray-Subramanian, Schanding, and Feeney-Kettler exceeded our expectations. *Early Childhood Education: A Practical Guide to Evidence-Based, Multitiered Service Delivery* provides an excellent resource for practitioners working in early childhood education. This book offers a process of working with young children, from screening to intervention, and includes numerous practical tools to enhance service delivery to this population. Screening, interventions, and progress monitoring resources are offered for both academic and social–emotional functioning. The authors go beyond individual interventions, and offer information regarding including and engaging families. We are pleased to have *Early Childhood Education: A Practical Guide to Evidence-Based, Multi-Tiered Service Delivery* as part of our series.

Finally, we want to extend our gratitude to Ms. Anna Moore and Routledge Publishing for their ongoing support of a book series focused on enriching the practice and service delivery within school settings. Their openness to meet the needs of school-based practitioners made the *School-Based Practice in Action* series possible. In addition, we must thank Mr. Dana Bliss, whose interest and collaboration made our idea for a book series a reality. We hope that you enjoy reading and implementing the materials in this book and the rest of the series as much as we have enjoyed working with the authors on developing these resources. Best wishes in your work with schools, children, and families.

Rosemary B. Mennuti, EdD, NCSP
Ray W. Christner, PsyD, NCSP
Series Editors, School-Based Practice in Action Series

An Introduction to Evidence-Based Early Childhood Education Practice Within a Multitiered Service Delivery Model

According to the 2010 Census, there were over 12 million children between the ages of 3 and 5 years old (U.S. Bureau of the Census, 2010). More children now access early childhood education services than ever before. In the mid- to late-1960s, between 10 and 16% of children between the ages of 3 and 4 were enrolled in school. Currently, over half of all 3- to 4-year-olds attend school (U.S. Department of Commerce, 2010). Early childhood programming has been shown to decrease grade retentions and placement in special education settings (Anderson et al., 2003). Now, more than ever, educational systems have the opportunity to directly intervene with children at an earlier age than was previously the case to prevent, identify, and treat childhood disabilities related to communication, learning, behavioral, and socioemotional difficulties.

Many children already receive services within early childhood settings. According to the U.S. Department of Education (2010), approximately 734,692 children between the ages of 3 and 5 have a disability and receive services under the Individuals with Disabilities Education Improvement Act, Part B (IDEA; 2004). These disabilities include developmental delays, autism spectrum disorders, intellectual disabilities, behavioral disorders, and health impairments. Systematic, data-based procedures are necessary to ensure that these children with disabilities, and those who struggle from time to time, receive the highest quality services to reach their full potential.

Multitiered Systems of Supports

Several models of service delivery have been proposed to enhance evidence-based practices within school settings. Response-to-intervention (Burns & Gibbons, 2012) and positive behavior intervention supports (Sailor, Dunlap, Sugai, & Horner, 2009) are two prominent models subsumed within the term *multitiered systems of supports* (MTSS). *Multitiered systems of supports* is an all-encompassing term that describes a data-based problem-solving approach to address the academic and behavioral (social/emotional) needs of students. This model incorporates the multiple tiers of varying intensity of instructional techniques and interventions.

Core Principles of MTSS. Several principles constitute the basis of MTSS. First, all children are capable of learning and achieving. Utilizing high-quality instruction, all children are able to make progress toward appropriate academic and behavioral goals. This first core principle supports a holistic view of child development (i.e., language, cognition, social-emotional, and motor). Second, learning should encompass both academic and behavioral goals. Incorporating public health perspectives (e.g., screening, prevention services) related to academic performance and behavioral issues is likely to provide school districts with optimal data to address all students' needs (Shapiro, 2000; Strein, Hoagwood, & Cohn, 2003). Next, service delivery is based on a collaborative model. This includes students, parents, teachers, administrators, instructional support staff, school psychologists, and other relevant school personnel. Additionally, MTSS is based on using data within a problem-solving model. All decisions are data-driven, collected from frequent assessments to closely monitor skills. Next, MTSS are based upon and supports future research and evidence-based practices.

Major Components of MTSS for Early Childhood. At the time of writing, there is no consensus regarding the "perfect" model of MTSS. The National Center for Learning Disabilities (2009) outlines the following components of an MTSS for early childhood:

- **Identification of the Child's Strengths and Needs: Screening, Assessment, and Progress Monitoring.** Universal screening to monitor and identify those needing additional assessments; assessment results that clearly identify strengths and needs related to his or her development; and progress monitoring over time to examine the effectiveness of the intensity of supports and services needed.

- **Evidence-Based Practices and Standard Protocols.** Use of practices supported by research and practitioner wisdom that are respectful of the family's values that increase the likelihood that the child will benefit from services. This includes the use of research-based, manualized interventions.
- **Fidelity of Implementation.** A high degree of adherence to instructional, intervention, and other support services as they are intended to be delivered.
- **Collaborative Problem Solving.** Inclusion of parents, teachers, and related service providers to define and analyze the problem, as well as develop and implement a support plan while evaluating its effectiveness.
- **Parental and Family Engagement.** Recognition that parents are essential to the success of their child and an emphasis on support for the entire family unit.

Overview of MTSS

The following conceptualization is based on the Kansas State Department of Education's (2010) integration of MTSS and RTI. Various recommendations for the number of tiers have been offered, with most conceptualized within three tiers: Tier 1—General Instruction, Universal Screening, and Progress Monitoring; Tier 2—Supplemental Instruction, Interventions, and Progress Monitoring; and Tier 3—Customized Instruction and Assessment. Tier 1 is comprised of the general curriculum that all students encounter. The curriculum should be comprehensive and evidence-based. Additionally, universal screening and assessment data are collected to identify those students making adequate progress and those who may be experiencing difficulties. Through progress monitoring, decisions are then made as to whether the child should receive additional instruction or monitoring. Tier 1 instructional practices alone are likely to benefit approximately 80% of children.

Within Tier 2, more intensive support is provided to small groups of children identified as in need of support from Tier 1 assessments. At this point, students within Tier 2 receive more frequent progress monitoring (at least once a month typically) while parents and school team members work collaboratively to resolve the concern. These interventions may include groups of three to five students and are delivered within the general education context. It is estimated that approximately 15% of children would be in need of Tier 2 services.

Tier 3 services are provided for those children who do not make the anticipated improvements after receiving Tier 2 interventions. While progress monitoring and the problem-solving model guide the process, the interventions are most individualized and intensive at this level, possibly leading to one-on-one support for the child. Tier 3 services does not necessarily mean a child would qualify for or need special education services; however, many children at this point may receive a comprehensive evaluation to determine if they would qualify for special education services due to a disability and educational need. Typically 5% of children would require Tier 3 services.

Surrounding all students are the components of best educational practices; that is, high-quality instruction, an evidence-based curriculum, and appropriate assessments. After selecting a curriculum supported by research, highly trained teachers can then demonstrate their effectiveness by utilizing various assessments to monitor student learning, adjusting instructional

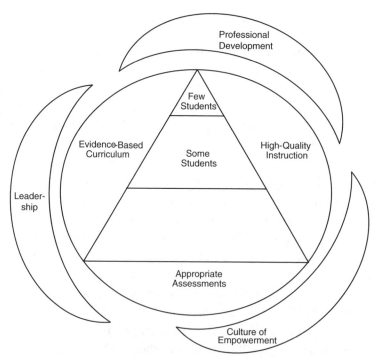

FIGURE 1.1 *Multi-Tier System of Supports (adapted from the Kansas State Department of Education).*

practices when necessary. These components cannot be achieved without ongoing support. Classroom, school building, district, and community leaders must support the activities within the model. Professional development must be provided to allow all involved in the process to increase skills, which in turn leads to the empowerment of students, parents, teachers, and support personnel.

Responsibility for MTSS: General Education or Special Education

Though MTSS may serve as a process to identify students who require special education, the primary responsibility rests with the general education setting. To this end, teachers, administrators, and other school personnel must learn how to collect and interpret data, link intervention to assessment data, and deliver evidence-based interventions. However, special education personnel will still be involved in the process, as MTSS crosses the general and special education settings. Students identified with a disability and receiving special education services are routinely monitored to determine their needs, the goal of which is to provide services in the least restrictive environment (possibly within general education). Hence, both general and special educators will need to create a clear channel of communication with parents to ensure that children are receiving the appropriate services to reach their full potential.

Current Applications of MTSS to Early Childhood Settings

Today more than ever, school systems are pressed to maximize student achievement and success. Meeting the needs of an increasingly culturally and linguistically diverse student population requires innovation and a reliance on utilizing evidence-based practices to maximize the effectiveness of school-based personnel and resources. The current focus for most work within MTSS has been on school-aged children; however, MTSS continues to garner attention related to younger children. The emphasis of MTSS on prevention and early identification of students with special needs aligns well with the efforts of early childhood education to address young children's development in the academic, social, and emotional areas.

Though still in its infancy, research is growing related to the development of tiered service models for pre-K students. Several sites around the United States have begun implementation of an MTSS. Currently, various groups such as university/research groups, state departments of education, and local school districts are working to further knowledge of challenges in MTSS within early childhood settings, such as assessments, professional development, intervention, implementation, and outcomes.

The Literacy Partnership. In Washington, DC, the U.S. Department of Education funded the Literacy Partnership as an Early Reading First project. The Literacy Project utilizes a three-tiered problem-solving model focused primarily on prevention of language and learning difficulties. Within Tier 1, literacy mentors and speech-language pathologists conducted assessments at the beginning and end of each school year to provide professional development and assisted teachers in personalizing classroom instruction. Parents received a semiannual family workshop focused on home literacy activities. At Tier 2, children identified as at risk from Tier 1 (or with known risk factors) participated in small-group instruction led by speech-language pathologists. This small-group intervention focused on vocabulary enhancement and phonological awareness. Those students progressing to the third tier were referred for a comprehensive evaluation and received intensive services from the literacy mentors or speech-language pathologists. Assessment results were reviewed biweekly by the team. According to a report from the National Center for Learning Disabilities (2009), Tier 1 and 2 activities improved students' performance on language and emergent literacy measures. Teacher performance, as observed by the Early Language and Literacy Classroom Observation, improved as well.

Recognition and Response. Recognition & Response (R&R) is a tiered program previously implemented at pilot sites in Florida and Maryland (National Center for Learning Disabilities, 2009). Developed by a research team at the University of North Carolina-Chapel Hill, R&R is an adaption of school-age MTSS (Coleman, Buysse, & Neitzel, 2006). Assessment is conducted under the "Recognition" component; all children undergo universal screening and then periodic progress monitoring in early language, literacy, and math. For "Response," core instruction is provided to all children, while targeted interventions are provided in Tier 2 and 3 to support children's learning. In evaluating the results, parents, teachers, specialists collaboratively work together to plan and evaluate students' progress within each tier. One distinguishing feature of R&R is its focus on examining instruction with dual language learners.

Center for Response to Intervention in Early Childhood (CRTIEC). Partnering with Kansas, Minnesota, Ohio, and Oregon, CRTIEC's goal is to reduce the prevalence of children not yet ready for kindergarten (National Center for Learning Disabilities, 2009). CRTIEC, led by Drs. Judith Carta and Charles Greenwood at the University of Kansas, is working to further knowledge related to assessments of language and early literacy within MTSS and further the evidence-base of Tier 2 and 3 interventions. One of the advances of CRTIEC is the implementation and improvement of the individual growth and development indicators (IGDIs). IGDIs are brief assessment instruments that measure early literacy and language, such as picture naming, alliteration, rhyming, and letter sounds. Based on this data, children can be screened and further progress monitored to determine the need for more intensive services. Screenings occur quarterly for all Tier 1 students and biweekly to progress monitor those students receiving interventions in Tier 2 or 3.

The Pyramid Model. Fox and colleagues have developed one of the few programs utilizing an MTSS model focusing on the social, emotional, and behavioral development of children. The pyramid model (Fox, Carta, Strain, Dunlap, & Hemmeter, 2010) incorporates a three-tiered model; however, Tier 1 emphasizes two universal components: (a) nurturing and responsive caregiving relationships (considered as the family or primary caregiver and the teacher) and (b) high-quality supportive environments (including both the home and community setting to be predictable and supportive). Within these supportive, positive relationships, adults can reduce the occurrence of challenging behaviors. Within Tier 2, children are explicitly taught about emotions, such as happiness, anger, and sadness. Children are taught how to control and appropriately express feelings related to anger, impulsivity, and frustration. For those children with the most severe social, emotional, and behavioral needs, Tier 3 utilizes a team approach to conduct a functional assessment of the child's challenging behavior to lead to the development of an individualized plan to meet the child's needs at home and school.

Rockford Early Childhood Program. The Rockford Public Schools Early Childhood Program has sought to incorporate MTSS to address both academic and behavioral goals. According to a report in the National Center for Learning Disabilities (2009), the Rockford Early Childhood Program committee responsible for MTSS includes an administrator, the early childhood special education supervisor, curriculum implementers, a social worker, classroom teachers (including a bilingual teacher), and a special education resource teacher. Within Tier 1, academic and behavioral curricula are taught, with all children entering the pre-K program screened prior to entry. Additional universal screening is conducted four times per year. Data teams and educational teams meet at least monthly to review progress for groups of students and individual students if necessary. Members on these teams include a variety of individuals such as parents, teachers, paraprofessionals, family support staff, social workers, psychologists, and administrators. The involvement of the family within the process is considered key. As noted in the report to the National Center for Learning Disabilities, 86 to 93% of students have demonstrated proficient ratings across areas based on the Illinois Early Learning Standards.

Colorado State Department of Education. The Colorado State Department of Education promotes the use of MTSS at the Pre-K level, adopting a three-tiered approach that has been implemented with school-age students for over 10 years (National Center for Learning Disabilities, 2009). The Colorado Department of Education (2008) provides a guidebook discussing the components of MTSS, with suggestions for working with gifted and talented students, English language learners, and preschool children. In formalizing Tier 1, all districts use one of three statewide-approved curricula. Additionally, some Colorado schools partner with other agencies such as Head Start programs and Child Care programs in creating a problem-solving process, stages of the MTSS, assignment of roles of individuals at various time points, and information to be shared with parents.

Summary

At this point, the public education system is in the best position ever to work with families to create positive outcomes for our nation's youngest learners. More children now than ever are enrolling in early education settings, allowing us to prevent and identify academic and behavioral difficulties. With the advent of MTSS within early childhood education settings, children and families will have the most advanced screenings and data to link assessment information to the most effective evidence-based interventions.

As seen from an initial review of some programs across the United States, there is no one MTSS model, and future models may look dramatically different from those used with school-aged children. Absent any federal mandate, each state and district will have to work to identify those procedures that can be incorporated or improved upon to enhance instruction and improve outcomes for children. At the core of these practices is a recognition of the child's strengths and weaknesses through collaborative problem-solving, evidence-based practices implemented with fidelity, and a focus on families to support the development of their child.

The following chapters will provide an overview of best practices and up-to-date information related to the delivery of MTSS to children and families within early childhood education. A review of relevant legal and practice guidelines related to early childhood education will be presented. Detailed information will be provided related to academic and behavioral assessments and interventions at various tiers, with special consideration given to culturally and linguistically diverse children and families.

2

The Law, Ethical Standards, and Guidelines for MTSS in Early Childhood Education

Within the field of education, there is an ongoing emphasis on improving access to, and quality of, education for all students. The provision of education is a power delegated to each state, but the federal government has recognized the importance of supporting states in this mission. This chapter will focus on some of the key federal laws that support the implementation of MTSS within early childhood settings. Additionally, professional groups also have great influence in shaping practice. Early childhood teacher associations as well as other professional organizations create ethical codes and guidelines that work in concert to self-regulate practice as well as inspire professionals to engage in best practices. An overview of these documents will be included in this chapter.

Legal Frameworks for Early Childhood Education and MTSS

Individuals with Disabilities Education Improvement Act (IDEA; 2004)

The 10th Amendment of the Constitution of the United States forbids the creation of a national school system, delegating the responsibility for education to state governments that, in turn, give authority to local school boards. In recognition of the importance of education, the federal government supports states by providing money contingent on compliance with federal law. The Individuals with Disabilities Education Improvement Act (IDEA, 2004) is one of those laws.

Public Law 94-142 was passed in 1975, and it focused on providing access to a free, appropriate public education for school-aged children with disabilities. Eleven years later, passage of PL 99-457 extended the same set of rights and protections to children between the ages of 3 and 5. In recognition that some of the disability categories outlined in the original law may not be applicable to or appropriate for younger children, Congress allowed states to incorporate an additional category of developmental delay or another non-categorical eligibility label. Currently reauthorized as the Individuals with Disabilities Education Improvement Act (IDEA, 2004), the law provides funds to state and local education agencies to ensure each child's educational needs, requiring agencies to conduct a full evaluation in all areas of suspected disability. If it is determined that a student has a disability that has an adverse effect on his or her educational progress, an Individual Education Program (IEP) must be developed. The IEP outlines the goals for the student, as well as the resources necessary (e.g., service providers, necessary materials, etc.) to reach those goals.

Under the most recent reauthorization of IDEA (2004), there has been a shift toward providing interventions early in addition to high quality instruction, to identify students with academic or behavioral disabilities. This is in contrast to a more traditional model of identifying the discrepancy that was previously used to identifying specific learning disabilities. The mandate states:

SEC.614. Evaluation, Eligibility Determinations, Individualized Education Programs, and Educational Placements (b) Evaluation Procedures—(6) Specific Learning Disabilities.—

(A) IN GENERAL.—Notwithstanding section 607(b), when determining whether a child has a specific learning disability as defined in section 602 (29), a local educational agency shall *not be required to take into consideration whether a child has a severe discrepancy between achievement and intellectual ability* [emphasis added] in oral expression, listening comprehension, written expression, basic reading skill, reading comprehension, mathematical calculation, or mathematical reasoning.

(B) ADDITIONAL AUTHORITY.—In determining whether a child has a specific learning disability, *a local educational agency may use a process that determines if the child responds to scientific, research-based intervention as a part of the evaluation procedures* [emphasis added] described in paragraphs (2) and (3).

MTSS fulfills the requirements of IDEA by incorporating the use of research-based interventions within the tiered supports. The passage and subsequent reauthorizations of IDEA have had a profound impact on providing resources to districts throughout the United States. With the most current reauthorization, up to 15% of IDEA funds are to be used for early intervention for students between the ages of 3 and 21 who do not have a disability, but may be in need of additional academic and behavioral support to be successful in the general education setting. In addition to IDEA, other initiatives have been passed to support early childhood education and MTSS.

No Child Left Behind (2001)

The No Child Left Behind Act (NCLB; 2001) is the most current reauthorization of the Elementary and Secondary Education Act. The primary purpose is to ensure that all children obtain a high-quality education and reach (at minimum) proficiency on state academic standards. Although much of the standards related to NCLB focus on school-aged children, specific provisions provide support for early childhood education: Early Reading First and Even Start.

Early Reading First. Given the fundamental contribution of reading in education, the Early Reading First initiative supports the creation of early childhood centers of excellence that work to prepare young children (especially those from low-income backgrounds) to enter kindergarten with requisite skills in language, cognition, and early reading skills. Through early screening of preschool children, the program seeks to increase a young child's oral language, phonological awareness, print awareness, and alphabetic knowledge through scientifically based reading research. In one evaluation report to Congress, the Early Reading First initiative was reported to have positive outcomes related to children's print and letter knowledge, but not on phonological awareness or oral language (Jackson et al., 2007).

Even Start. The William F. Goodling Even Start Family Literacy Program (Even Start) offers grants that support family literacy projects. First funded in 1988, the program is currently reauthorized by the Literacy Act of 2000 and NCLB 2001. Four major components of family literacy are addressed by Even Start: (a) early childhood education, (b) adult literacy, (c) parenting education, and (d) interactive literacy activities for parents and children. With a focus on family collaboration and building relationships with government agencies, universities, public schools, Head Start programs, and other stakeholders, Even Start embodies several characteristics of MTSS, such as collaborative family involvement and a culture of empowering individuals.

Section 5542 of NCLB. In addition to literacy efforts promoted in early childhood by NCLB, funding is available for agencies to promote emotional and social development. Section 5542 of NCLB provides funding for programs that work to address the needs of children (from birth to 7 years old) and families related to mental health, physical health, substance abuse, educational, domestic violence prevention, child welfare, and social services. As part of this funding mechanism, agencies are encouraged to develop or enhance community partnerships to provide supports for children and families.

Further Federal Resources

Race to the Top—Early Learning Challenge. Created as part of the American Recovery and Reinvestment Act of 2009, Race to the Top—Early Learning Challenge (RTT-ELC) works in concert with previously reviewed federal programs to close the achievement gap for children at risk. From this program, states are provided grants of up to $100 million to increase the number of young children enrolled in high-quality early childhood education programs, design and implement an integrated system of early education and services (e.g., MTSS), and ensure appropriate use of assessments for early childhood. For the 2011 fiscal year, nine states were awarded grants. The RTT-ELC focuses on five key domains. The first goal is the establishment or improvement of coordination among state programs and agencies to ensure consistency and sustainability of early learning and development. Each state granted an award works toward creating a rating and improvement system to document program quality. Third, supporting professionals within early childhood is of major importance. RTT-ELC works to further train personnel by providing professional development, career advancement opportunities, and standards related to knowledge and competence of early childhood educators. Fourth, common standards and assessments will be developed to address the unique learning, behavioral, and health needs of children, with a focus on family support as well. Finally, states must measure outcomes and progress related to the readiness of children entering kindergarten.

Ethical Standards Related to MTSS in Early Childhood Education

Standards for Educational and Psychological Testing

Much responsibility is placed on individuals involved in the assessment and decision-making process related to eligibility, progress monitoring, and service delivery. The American Educational Research Association (AERA), the American Psychological Association (APA), and the National Council on Measurement in Education (NCME) collaborated to jointly publish a comprehensive set of standards to guide practitioners from various fields involved in assessment. Given the importance of assessment data collected within MTSS, it is imperative for practitioners to be well-versed in understanding the psychometric properties of instruments they use.

The *Standards for Educational and Psychological Testing* (AERA, APA, & NCME, 1999) is broken into three sections: (a) test construction, evaluation, and documentation; (b) fairness in testing; and (c), testing applications. Section I covers various psychometric issues faced in assessment (i.e., validity, reliability, measurement error, test development/revision, scales, norms, and comparability of scores) and outlines proper procedures for test administration, scoring, reporting, and how best to provide supporting documentation for tests. Section II outlines issues related to rights and responsibilities of test takers, with two chapters devoted to testing individuals from diverse linguistic backgrounds and individuals with disabilities. Given the growing cultural and linguistic diversity of children within the United States, these issues will become more pronounced in the coming years. Section III outlines responsibilities of test users and standards specific to psychological and educational testing and assessment. Additionally, standards related to testing in employment, credentialing, program evaluation, and public policy are outlined. An updated version of the Standards is planned for late 2012 or early 2013.

Professional Organizations' Guidelines for Practice

Several professional groups recognize and promote the use of evidence-based practices, one of the core components of MTSS. What follows is a brief overview of the need for evidence-based practices from various stakeholder organizations involved in early childhood education.

National Association for the Education of Young Children (NAEYC)

The NAEYC is the world's largest organization working on behalf of children from birth through age 8. Members include teachers, paraeducators, administrators, university faculty, families, and others interested in early childhood education. NAEYC also provides accreditation and monitors standards for early childhood education programs to ensure the highest quality. In addition, the organization has created several position papers that may guide professionals practice within early childhood programs.

The position statement, *Developmentally Appropriate Practice in Early Childhood Programs Serving Children from Birth through Age 8,* which was adopted in 2009, promotes a framework for what is considered best practice (NAEYC, 2009a). Aligned with principles from the MTSS model, NAEYC affirms that best practice is based on research, not assumptions related to curriculum and teacher effectiveness. In striving to close the achievement gap among various student groups, NAEYC recognizes that early childhood programs must provide additional learning experiences for children who are struggling or at risk of failing (i.e., supplemental, research-based instruction and interventions). In improving education, they promote better alignment between educational systems, incorporating strategies based on preschool and elementary-grade practices. NAEYC acknowledges the need for effective teachers who are trained to adapt curriculum to meet the needs of their young learners, promoting ongoing professional development, sufficient support, and appropriate compensation. Additionally, NAEYC recognizes the importance of addressing culturally and linguistic diversity in young children (NAEYC, 2009b; see Table 2.1).

Council for Exceptional Children

The Council for Exceptional Children (CEC) is an international professional association dedicated to issues surrounding the success of individuals with disabilities or gifts or talents. The CEC is composed of 17 divisions, with one division focused on early childhood, and seeks to advocate for public policy, professional standards, and professional development to promote effective practice.

In their effort to support evidence-based practice, the CEC has developed a manual to assist in the classification of such practices (CEC, 2008). An evidence-based practice is defined as "a systematic analysis of relevant research on a targeted practice to determine the quality of the evidence base." Based

TABLE 2.1 NAEYC Recommendations for Working with Culturally and Linguistically Diverse Children and Families*

Working with	Recommendations
Families	Actively involve families within your program.
	Help families realize the advantages of being bilingual/multilingual; provide strategies to support, maintain, and preserve the language and culture at home.
Young Children	Ensure family's cultural values are honored.
	Ensure children remain cognitively, linguistically, and emotionally connected to their home language and culture.
	Encourage home language and literacy development to assist with English language proficiency.
	Help develop essential learning concepts within the child's first language and cultural contexts.
	Develop alternative, creative strategies to promote all children's participation and learning.
	Provide multiple ways for children to show what they know and can do.
Early Childhood Professionals	Provide continuing education related to culture, language, and diversity.
	Recruit and support educators who reflect diverse backgrounds.

*Based on NAEYC (2009b)

on the review of the research literature, a practice may be classified into three categories: (a) Positive Evidence-Base, (b) Insufficient Evidence-Base, or (c) Negative Evidence-Base. Within the Insufficient category, three subcategories are possible. A practice may be considered as having a Potentially Positive, Mixed Effects, or No Discernible Effects Evidence Base. Additionally, the CEC publishes articles regarding evidence-based practices and the journal *TEACHING Exceptional Children* (published by the CEC) identified six evidence-based practices for children with an autism spectrum disorder (Ryan, Hughes, Katsiyannis, McDaniel, & Sprinkle, 2011).

In addressing the creation of new models to implement in early childhood education, several organizations—the CEC's Division for Early Childhood (DEC), the NAEYC, and the National Head Start Association (NHSA)—are working together to create a joint position statement related to MTSS (NAEYC, DEC, & NHSA, 2012). Though still in draft form, four key features are described: (a) multitiers of instruction; (b) a high quality curriculum; (c) ongoing assessment and progress monitoring; and (d) collaborative problem solving. The draft reiterates the lack of extensive research regarding the use of tiered frameworks in addressing the needs of young children, especially infants and toddlers. The organizations call for additional research related to the impact of instructional practices and outcomes for these populations, noting the need for adequate assessment instruments and how to use that data. Finally, the organizations note the challenges that will come in the possible confounding of the implementation of tiered instructional services and referrals to special education.

National Professional Development Center on Inclusion

More research has been focused on developing MTSS with school-aged children. There is also the recognition that MTSS will likely include several iterations across states and educational settings. With those ideas in mind, the National Professional Development Center on Inclusion (NPDCI; dedicated to providing technical support to teachers educating young children with disabilities and their typically developing peers) has proposed a framework for Response-to-Intervention, which can be incorporated into an MTSS model (NPDCI, 2012). The model reinforces the use of formative assessments to gather data on the child's behavior and academic competencies. Included within these assessments are universal screening and progress monitoring. The second key component includes an effective core curriculum, with tiered interventions and support—core curriculum, targeted small-group interventions, and intensive individualized interventions/support. The third key component reiterates the need for collaborative, decision-based decision making. Practitioners must work with families, specialists, and others to assess, interpret, and build comprehensive educational programs for young learners.

American Psychological Association and National Association of School Psychologists

The American Psychological Association (APA) is the largest organization representing psychology in the United States. Psychologists involved with the treatment of children and families seek to improve the education, health, and welfare of children and families. As such, the APA has developed a set of guidelines related to evidence-based practice, defined as "the integration of the best available research with clinical expertise in the context of patient characteristics, culture, and preferences" (APA Task Force, 2006, p. 273). Recognizing the vast sources of knowledge, research designs may include clinical observations, qualitative research, systematic case studies/single-case experimental designs, public health and ethnographic research, process-outcome studies, randomized clinical trials, studies delivered in natural settings, and meta-analyses. In addition to research, clinical expertise is highlighted. Clinical expertise (i.e., an individual's education, training, and experience) combined with knowledge and skill in implementing empirically supported interventions combine to provide the optimal treatment for children and families within MTSS. Some final, but important, considerations are characteristics of the learner, culture, and preferences. These factors figure prominently with early childhood education such as examining the child's and family's background, cultural and linguistic influences, and preferences for goals and services.

The National Association of School Psychologists (NASP; dedicated to preparing school psychologists to enhance the learning and mental health of all children) recognizes the importance of early childhood educational experiences. In their position paper on *Early Intervention Services* (NASP, 2003), early intervention is emphasized because it can have a positive impact on a child's future academic success and positive social, emotional, and behavioral development. The NASP encourages its members to advocate at the national, state, and local levels for early intervention services for those young children with disabilities and those at-risk. As initially noted by the NAEYC, the NASP also promotes developmentally appropriate practices to address a child's unique strengths and needs. Following along with recommendations from other organizations, family involvement is considered crucial, and school psychologists are required to recognize cultural and linguistic diversity. As school psychologists may function in the role of assessment personnel, a separate position paper was adopted regarding early childhood assessment (NASP, 2009). School psychologists' assessments within early childhood settings should be designed to detect the need for intervention, enhance service delivery, and enhance program and system effectiveness. This paper emphasizes the importance of universal screening, examining the ecology of the classroom, utilizing formative data such as progress monitoring, and collecting data related to intervention fidelity. School psychologists are also tasked with selecting technically adequate measurement tools (such as those meeting requirements outlined in the *Standards for Educational and Psychological Testing* (American Educational Research Association [AERA], American Psychological Association [APA], & National Council on Measurement in Education [NCME], 1999), obtaining data from multiple methods, modalities, and informants. Finally, the data collected as part of early childhood education should facilitate a child's transition into kindergarten.

Summary

As previously discussed here and in Chapter 1, the model of MTSS in early childhood settings is a work in progress. Multiple factors will influence the final conceptual frameworks, and it is likely that MTSS models will vary across states and educational settings. Education in the United States is the responsibility of each state. State governments will be primary sources for determining the development of MTSS within early childhood education; however, the federal government recognizes the need to support states in providing a quality education. Federal funding laws, such as the IDEA (2004) and components of the NCLB (2001), provide money to states in return for following certain mandates and restrictions.

Another way MTSS may be influenced in the future is through groups of professionals setting ethical standards. A clear example of multiple disciplines working to shape the standards of a field is the publication of the *Standards for Educational and Psychological Testing*. Standards related to choosing assessments based on reliability, validity, and nondiscriminatory practices have been agreed upon by major organizations interested in education, psychology, and measurement.

Finally, various professional organizations have provided specific guidance in developing, adopting, and implementing MTSS within early childhood settings. Given the diverse organizations presented in this chapter, there appears to be a strong consensus regarding the general components of MTSS (typically based on models of Response-to-Intervention). As disciplines progress and more research becomes available related to outcomes of MTSS, families and educational professionals will improve their abilities to meet the needs of all early learners.

3

Universal Screening
of Early Academic Skills

onsider the case of Sherman Academy. Sherman is a small preschool in a large metropolitan city. Serving children 18 months to 6 years old, Sherman offers language enrichment, therapeutic, arts, and academic programming. During recent team meetings, Sherman staff members have begun to express concerns about the extent to which current assessment practices are informing their delivery of academic, social, emotional, and behavioral supports. Consequently, the school is seeking guidance from an educational consultant and has begun to learn more about assessing their students' needs within a MTSS.

Universal screening of core academic skills is a cornerstone of multitiered service delivery models and would serve as a useful first step for Sherman Academy, as it offers an efficient means for periodically gathering snapshot data of all students' academic performance to identify students who may be at risk of academic difficulty (e.g., Burns & Gibbons, 2012). In the last several years, universal screening of reading outcomes at the elementary level has become well established, and more recently, schools have begun to integrate universal screening of math outcomes into their models. To date, universal screening of writing remains somewhat untouched. As well, universal screening in early childhood education and secondary settings is also in its infancy. This chapter begins with an overview of the general universal screening process that has been established at the elementary level, followed by a discussion of universal screening of early academic skills in early childhood education settings.

Overview of Universal Screening

Universal screening of academic skills typically occurs through the administration of general outcome measures (GOMs) during benchmark assessment periods that generally take place during the fall, winter, and spring of each school year. A GOM is a standardized measure designed to assess students' competencies in a curriculum by evaluating multiple skills in a given academic domain (Fuchs & Deno, 1991), and curriculum-based measurement (CBM) is one type of GOM often used during benchmark assessments (Deno, 1985). Ideally, universal screening provides systems-wide data that can be used to inform service delivery, and CBMs are particularly useful because they provide a valid and reliable means for educators to gather formative data about their students' academic progress in an efficient, cost-effective, and user-friendly manner that allows for comparisons within and across students, classrooms, grade levels, buildings, or districts (Burns & Gibbons, 2012). That is, by examining all students' performance as a whole, a school or school district may begin to better understand the effectiveness of the core curriculum in meeting students' instructional needs.

Several steps are involved in the universal screening process, and Burns and Gibbons (2012) provide a detailed description of these procedures in elementary and secondary schools. Deliberate and extensive planning must occur prior to the actual administration of selected screeners in a district. Educators first decide which domains will be assessed. As noted previously, universal screening of reading outcomes such as oral reading fluency and reading comprehension has become fairly well established. Some school districts also measure early literacy skills such as letter naming fluency, letter sound fluency, phoneme blending accuracy, phoneme segmentation accuracy, and nonsense word fluency in kindergarten and first grade. After determining the domains to be assessed, educators then select screening tools to meet student and district needs (an up-to-date overview of screening tools is available at the National Center on Response to Intervention website: http://www.rti4success.org/screeningTools). Finally, a timeframe in which to administer the screeners is selected (often the last two weeks of September, January, and May), a measurement team is established and trained, and the benchmark assessment takes place. With screening tools that are designed for group administration, such as math computation and reading comprehension CBMs, it is often appropriate and agreeable for teachers to be members of the measurement team and to conduct the benchmark assessments in their classrooms. However, given that many screening tools, such as oral reading fluency CBMs, are designed for individual administration, composing a measurement team of educators such as paraprofessionals, school psychologists, and perhaps university partners may better promote teacher acceptance of universal screening procedures.

Once the screening data are collected, target scores are then identified, the data are reviewed, and students who are performing below expected levels and are in need of additional academic supports are identified. As Burns and Gibbons (2012) explain, districts may decide to either use target scores (norm-referenced or criterion-referenced) or cut scores based on the local distribution of scores. Once this decision is made, and the data are initially reviewed (by the school psychologist, for example), the data are then also reviewed with the grade-level teachers to (a) set realistic and attainable goals for the next benchmark assessment period and (b) also make decisions about general service delivery to support all students and small-group or individualized service delivery to support students who performed below target levels.

Universal Screening in Preschool

Along with developmental screening, diagnostic assessment, progress monitoring, and program evaluation, universal screening is one type of assessment conducted in preschools. Although universal screening practices of early academic skills in preschools are less developed, the aforementioned practices can be used to inform the creation of universal screening procedures in preschools. One significant consideration in the creation of a universal screening process in preschools, as opposed to elementary and secondary schools, is the varied development of young children. Therefore, it may be useful to pair universal screening of early academic skills, as well as social-emotional and behavioral skills, with developmental screening. This section begins with a presentation of general considerations for developmental screening, followed by a review of the current state of universal screening for early literacy and math skills. The interested reader is referred to Brassard and Boehm (2007) for a complete discussion of developmental screening.

Developmental Screening. Developmental screening in preschools is quite common because it provides a means for identifying young children who may be at risk of later experiencing difficulties when academic, social-emotional, and behavioral demands increase in grade school (Brassard & Boehm, 2007). Developmental screening is also mandated by IDEA (2004) and can be used to measure physical, motor, cognitive, communicative, social, emotional, and adaptive development, with more emphasis generally being placed on physical, motor, cognitive, and communicative skills. Although screening practices generally focus on the child, Brassard and Boehm (2007) recommend factors related to family, interaction patterns, school practices, and prior interventions also be addressed during the developmental screening process.

Similar to the benchmark assessment process, a developmental screening program advances through multiple phases including planning, outreach, conducting the screening and integrating the results, communicating with parents, follow-up and prereferral intervention, and evaluation (Brassard & Boehm, 2007). Although screening processes are often similar in many ways (e.g., planning for screening and using results to inform practice/instruction), developmental screening differs from the typical benchmark assessment in at least two ways. First, the instruments used for developmental screening are generally designed to provide a measure of functioning across multiple domains of development, rather than in a single academic domain. For example, Brassard and Boehm (2007) note the *Early Screening Inventory—Revised* (ESI-R; Meisels, Marsden, Wiske, & Henderson, 1997) is one of the more useful instruments for screening preschool children. The ESI-R is a screening tool designed to measure visual, motor/adaptive, language and cognition, and gross motor development in children aged 3 to 6 years. Another difference can be noticed in a preschool's outreach efforts and family involvement. Through outreach, the school actively reaches out to families to make them aware of the school's screening program and to educate them about typical and atypical child development. Given the impact early intervention can have on the healthy development of young children, such outreach efforts are of paramount importance in the developmental screening process.

Instructional Screening. Consider the case of Sherman Academy: The staff share their developmental screening practices with the educational consultant and together determine that the process they have in place is meeting the developmental needs of their children, and the staff is more concerned about their assessment of early academic skills. Sherman offers academic instruction in preliteracy, prewriting, premath, science, and social studies for young children 3 to 5 years of age across three classrooms, first in a project-based format and later through more formal academic curricula, until students enter kindergarten. Currently, students' academic performance is assessed twice a year via pre- and postmeasures developed by each teacher and administered at the beginning and end of the school year. Historically, each classroom teacher has individually used the data to identify students who are achieving at expected levels, as well as significantly above and below the teacher's general expectations, and then has suggested tutoring or an extended day program for the students who are struggling the most. The teachers would like to have a more uniform method of evaluating their students, with the hope of using the data to inform instruction, so they are interested in learning more about universal screening.

In preschools, instructional screening is generally conducted via performance-based assessment such as criterion-referenced tests (CRTs), curriculum-based assessment and measurement (CBA and CBM, a form of CRT), and portfolio assessment (Brassard & Boehm, 2007). Although all of these techniques can, and arguably should, be used in the assessment of early academic skills, the efficiency and utility of CBM make it a more appropriate technique for universal screening of all young children in a preschool setting. Although CBMs are generally already quite child-friendly, characteristics that are especially important with CBMs used with young children include individual administration, minimal motor and linguistic requirements, demonstration and sample items, minimal within-task visual distractions, and minimal within-task child–examiner conversations (Floyd, Hojnoski, & Key, 2006). Of further note, CBMs are specifically designed to be used repeatedly to monitor academic progress, so preschools such as Sherman can conduct universal screenings of early literacy and math skills throughout the year and also monitor the progress of specific students more frequently.

Notwithstanding these attributes, CBM is particularly beneficial in universal screening because it provides a means for linking assessment to intervention/instruction, a specific goal of Sherman Academy. The following sections will provide an overview of CBMs designed specifically for use in the universal screening of preschool children's early literacy and math skills. The following content is also available on the companion *Early Childhood Education* website.

Universal Screening of Early Literacy Skills

Early, or emergent, literacy encompasses the attitudes, knowledge, and resulting skills children typically develop before receiving formal instruction in reading and writing (Whitehurst & Lonigan, 1998). In reading, early literacy skills include phonological awareness, print knowledge (including alphabet knowledge), and oral language. Given that these skills remain stable over time and are predictive of later reading ability, using universal screening to accurately identify children who may need additional support in fully developing early literacy skills is of paramount importance.

Preschool Individual Growth and Development Indicators (Preschool IGDIs). One of the most widely used screening tools for early literacy skills of preschool children is the *Preschool Individual Growth and Development Indicators* (Preschool IGDIs; Early Childhood Research Institute on Measuring Growth & Development [ECRI-MGD], 1998–2000). The preschool IGDIs were originally a set of three, standardized GOMs designed to assess early literacy skills of children 3 to 5 years of age (ECRI-MGD, 1998–2000). Picture Naming provides a measure of expressive language development, and Rhyming and Alliteration provide measures of phonological awareness. In addition, in an effort to improve and expand upon these measures, additional measures of alphabet knowledge and comprehension are currently being developed (Bradfield, Wackerle-Holman, & McConnell, 2011).

Originally developed through the Early Childhood Research Institute on Measuring Growth and Development (ECRI-MGD) at the University of Minnesota's Center for Early Education Development (CEED), the preschool IGDIs are research-based, and research supporting their use continues to be conducted by CEED and the Center for Response to Intervention in Early Childhood (CRTIEC). The preschool IGDIs can be administered by trained educators in approximately 10 minutes and are sensitive to small changes over time, making them ideal for universal screening periodically throughout the school year, as well as more frequent progress monitoring. Furthermore, Picture Naming has been shown to be effective in measuring the growth of early literacy skills in English of approximately 1,000 children who speak Somali, Hmong, and Spanish (Estrem, 2011; Estrem & McConnell, 2008). In addition, although Picture Naming can be administered in Spanish, at the time of this writing performance comparisons can only be made if local Spanish norms are created, and they have not yet been developed. The psychometric properties of the preschool IGDIs indicate moderate to strong test-retest reliability (Missall & McConnell, 2004), and preliminary national norms, based on a sample of over 7,000 typically developing preschoolers, have recently been reported (Roseth, Missal, & McConnell, 2012).

The myIGDIs website offers teachers and administrators free administration instructions, background literature, demonstration videos, and mobile applications (see www.myigdis.com). Online tools for data management and progress monitoring are also available through Early Learning Labs. In addition, given the continual advances with the Preschool IGDIs, updates can be found at the CEED website (http://www.cehd.umn.edu/ceed/projects/crtiec/default.html).

mCLASS+. Additional universal screening options include the mCLASS+ (formerly mCLASS CIRCLE; Wireless Generation, 2010); the *Early Arithmetic, Reading, and Learning Indicators for Preschool* (EARLI) literacy probes (DiPerna & Morgan, 2005); and the *Early Learning Observation and Rating Scale* (ELORS; Gillis, West, & Coleman, 2010a). Like the EL-IGDIs, the mCLASS+ and EARLI literacy probes are GOMs and are therefore suitable for progress monitoring as well as universal screening. The mCLASS+ literacy system (Wireless Generation, 2010) is a mobile version of the CIRCLE Phonological Awareness, Language, and Literacy System plus (C-PALLS+). mCLASS+ is based on the Center for Improving the Readiness of Children for Learning and Education (CIRCLE) framework developed by Dr. Susan Landry, as well as the research of the Children's Learning Institute (CLI). It addresses the early literacy and math needs of children 3.5 to 5 years of age and is composed of three components: assessment, grouping, and observables. Using data collected through assessment tasks, mCLASS+ facilitates the development of small groups to promote skill building as well as continued progress monitoring through observables. Assessment of early literacy involves measurement of phonological awareness, print knowledge, and oral language development. Universal screening via assessment tasks is recommended at the beginning, middle, and end of the school year with assessment tasks being administered as a universal screener (e.g., October 15 to November 15) followed by the administration of observables (e.g., November 15 to December 15) to monitor progress throughout the school year. Data to support the psychometric properties of mCLASS+ suggests it is technically adequate and sensitive to growth over time (Children's Learning Institute, 2009).

Administration requires a mobile device such as a PDA. During administration, the examiner may use an Onscreen Flipbook or a hard copy of the C-PALLS Flipbook, and the child's response is recorded on the mobile device. Rapid Letter Naming and Rapid Vocabulary Naming are administered for 60 seconds each. Phonological Awareness tasks are comprised of seven, untimed tasks that take approximately 10 minutes to administer to one child: Listening, Rhyming 1, Rhyming 2, Alliteration, Words in a Sentence, Syllabication, and Onset-Rime. Based on scores for each task, a child's level of understanding is categorized as Full Understanding, Some Understanding, or Emerging Understanding, and children demonstrating some or emerging understanding are then grouped accordingly based on the needs of each child. Assessment data are also directly linked to curriculum activities in a CIRCLE manual. mCLASS+ is available in English and Spanish and can be used to create individualized portfolios for each student, manage data for all students, and track progress over time. The Children's Learning Institute and Wireless Generation websites provide additional information and resources for mCLASS+ (see www.childrenslearninginstitute.org and www.wirelessgeneration.com).

Early Arithmetic, Reading, and Learning Indicators for Preschool (EARLI). The EARLI literacy probes (DiPerna & Morgan, 2005) are research-based GOMs specifically designed to facilitate the identification of the learning needs of preschool children. The probes are appropriate for children 3 to 5 years of age; require relatively little administration time; and are composed of six measures of early literacy that address phonological awareness, vocabulary, print knowledge, letter-name knowledge, and letter-sound knowledge: Alphabet Recitation, Letter Sounds, Sound Deletion, Letter Naming, Segmenting, and Expressive Vocabulary. For universal screening purposes, the literacy probes may be administered three times per year and more frequently as a measure of progress or response to intervention. Studies examining the technical adequacy of EARLI literacy probes suggest the probes are psychometrically sound and appropriate for use with culturally and linguistically diverse children in Head Start and other preschool settings and are sensitive to growth over time (Hochstedt, Lei, PiPerna, & Morgan, 2011; E. E. Reid, Morgan, DiPerna, & Lei, 2006; M. A. Reid, DiPerna, Morgan, & Lei, 2009).

During the administration of Alphabet Recitation, children are asked to recite the letters of the alphabet. During Letter Sounds, children are visually presented with letters and asked to verbally provide the correct sound. Administration of Letter Naming is similar, with children providing the correct letter name. During Sound Deletion, children listen to a word, mentally delete a sound, and verbally state the remaining sounds, and during Segmenting, children listen to a word and verbally state the beginning, middle, or end sound. Finally, during Expressive Vocabulary, children are presented with pictures and asked to name each picture. Administration is standardized, and all tasks are timed. To enhance standardization, Alphabet Recitation, Letter Sounds, Letter Naming, and Expressive Vocabulary can be presented via a slide-show presentation on a computer (Reid et al., 2009). The EARLI literacy probes are currently in development and have not been published. Interested practitioners and researchers may contact Dr. James DiPerna at Pennsylvania State University for additional information.

Early Learning Observation and Rating Scale (ELORS). The ELORS is a screening tool codeveloped by the National Center for Learning Disabilities and the Frank Porter Graham (FPG) Child Development Institute, and it differs from the aforementioned screeners in that it relies on observation and is not a GOM. Its development is aligned with preschool models of RTI, and it is designed to facilitate screening and progress monitoring of children 4 years of age by parents and teachers in seven domains the year before kindergarten: perceptual and motor, self-management, social and emotional, early math, early literacy, receptive language, and expressive language. With regard to early literacy, the ELORS provides a measure of a child's alphabet knowledge, Phonological Awareness, Syllables and Rhymes, Print and Book Knowledge, Prewriting Skills/Activities, Decoding, Word Recognition, and Letter Sounds Knowledge.

The ELORS is available in three forms: Whole Class, Teacher-Individual Child, and Parent-Individual Child. The Whole Class form is best suited for universal screening as it provides the teacher with a systematic way of observing students in the classroom, recording performance, and identifying students who may benefit from additional support in early literacy. Administration is generally conducted across a period of 1 or 2 weeks after children have been in school for at least one month. During this time period, the teacher observes behavior and makes note of the child's name and the particular behaviors of concern within each domain (e.g., Early Literacy). The teacher also notes the frequency of each behavior. At the end of the observation period, the teacher completes a Whole Class Observation Record, indicating the domains of concern for each child in the class. Results of the Whole Class form are then used to determine if an individual observation of any child is warranted. Results of the Whole Class form can also be used to identify class-wide areas of need. Theoretical and social validity has been demonstrated and further examination of reliability and validity is needed (Gillis, West, Coleman, 2010b).

Universal Screening of Early Math Skills

Early math skills include numbers and operations, geometry, patterns, cardinality, and others. Similar to early literacy skills, early math skills have been shown to be predictive of later math performance in elementary and secondary school (e.g., Jimerson, Egeland, & Teo, 1999; Stevenson & Newman, 1986). As such, universal screening can be instrumental in the identification of children who may benefit from additional supports.

mCLASS+. In addition to literacy tasks, another component of the mCLASS+ system is a math screener generally appropriate for children 3.5 to 5 years of age, although the screener has not been validated for use with children younger than 4 years old. Assessment of early math with the math screener involves measurement of counting, shape naming, operations, number identification, and shape discrimination. The math screener is designed to be administered as a universal screener within the same timeframe as the mCLASS+ literacy tasks.

Like the literacy probes, administration requires a mobile device such as a PDA. During administration, the examiner may use an Onscreen Flipbook or a hard copy of the C-PALLS Flipbook, and the child's response is recorded on the mobile device. Specific tasks include Rote Counting, Shape Naming, Number Discrimination, Number Naming, Shape Discrimination, Set Counting, and Operations, and total administration time is approximately 5 minutes. The math screener does not measure patterning skills. Following administration, children are assigned to groups and specific curriculum activities based on their performance.

Prekindergarten Early Numeracy Screener. The Pre-Kindergarten Early Numeracy Screener was developed through the work of VanDerHeyden, Broussard, Fabre et al. (2004) and is a set of six GOMs designed to measure number identification, counting, and visual discrimination skills of children 4 years of age via Number Selection, Number Naming, Counting Objects, Free Count, Discrimination Tasks, and Choosing Shapes. Administration time is brief, and the measures are designed to be administered as universal screeners three times per year and more often to monitor progress of students in need of additional supports. Technical adequacy has been established for four of the measures; however, further research must be conducted to determine if the Choose Shape and Free Count measures are appropriate for use with young children (VanDerHeyden, Broussard, & Cooley, 2006; VanDer-Heyden, Broussard, Fabre et al., 2004).

During administration, children meet individually with an examiner and are asked to complete a variety of tasks such as counting aloud; counting objects; naming numbers; selecting numbers; selecting shapes; and discriminating among numbers, letters, and shapes. Fluency scores are then calculated based on their performance. Following administration, scores can be entered into an online data management system. Additional information about the Pre-Kindergarten Early Numeracy Screener is available through the System to Enhance Educational Performance (STEEP) website (see www.isteeplearning.com).

Preschool Numeracy Indicators (PNIs). The PNIs are a set of nine GOMs designed to measure the development of number and operations, geometry, pattern completion, and cardinality skills of children 3 to 6 years of age in a brief period of time. The original PNIs consisted of four tasks assessing number and operations development: One-to-One Counting, Oral Counting, Number Naming, and Quantity Comparison (Floyd, Hojnoski, & Key, 2006). More recently, the following additional tasks assessing geometry were field-tested: Shape Naming Fluency, Shape Selection Fluency, and Shape Composition. Pattern completion skills are assessed via Pattern Completion, and cardinality skills are assessed via Cardinality. The PNIs are appropriate for use across ages and can be administered repeatedly for the purposes of universal screening or progress monitoring. Examinations of the technical adequacy of the PNIs are ongoing and suggest all tasks besides Pattern Completion are psychometrically sound and sensitive to growth over time with diverse populations and in diverse settings (Floyd et al., 2006; R. L. Hojnoski, personal communication, May 21, 2012; Hojnoski, Silberglitt, & Floyd, 2009; Polignano & Hojnoski, 2012). However, given that the growth rate is small, it is recommended that the PNIs be administered as universal screeners no more than three times per year (Hojnoski et al., 2009).

During individual administration, children complete nine measures. During the administration of tasks measuring skills related to number and operations, children are asked to count aloud, count circles printed on a sheet of paper, name numbers, and select the set of circles that has the greatest number of circles. During the administration of geometry measures, children are asked to name shapes, select shapes, and identify and name shapes presented in a composite picture. During Pattern Completion, the examiner visually and orally presents children with primary-colored AB, ABBA, and ABC patterns and asks the child to identify what comes next. Finally, during Cardinality, children are asked to count the number of circles printed on a page and then answer the question, "How many circles did you count?" Fluency scores are then calculated for each task. The PNIs are currently in development and have not been published, but are being used in several states. Interested practitioners and researchers may contact Dr. Robin Hojnoski at Lehigh University for additional information.

Early Arithmetic, Reading, and Learning Indicators for Preschool (EARLI). In addition to probes of early literacy, EARLI math measures assessing number identification, counting, and basic arithmetic were also developed by Reid, DiPerna, Morgan, and Lei (2006; Lei, Wu, DiPerna, & Morgan, 2009). As with EARLI literacy probes, EARLI math probes are brief and were designed to be administered during universal screening and for progress monitoring. Further, examination of the probes' psychometric properties shows evidence of technical adequacy (Reid et al., 2006).

During the administration, children complete six measures: Counting Aloud, Number Naming, Counting Objects, Grouping, Pattern Recognition, and Measurement. Via these brief tasks, children count aloud, name numerals presented visually, count objects, quickly identify the number of objects in a group, identify pattern sequences, and identify measurement concepts such as taller and shorter. The EARLI math probes are currently in development and have not been published. Interested practitioners and researchers may contact Dr. James DiPerna at Pennsylvania State University for additional information.

Early Learning Observation and Rating Scale (ELORS). Although the ELORS relies on observation and is not a GOM, as noted previously, it does have an early math component that allows parents and teachers to screen early math skills in children 3 to 5 years of age (Gillis, West, & Coleman, 2010a, 2010b). Specifically, the ELORS facilitates measurement quantity comparison, one-to-one correspondence, concept of attribute, recognition of simple patterns and sequences, spatial orientation, concept of time, counting, concept of number, number recognition, and number naming. Administration procedures are aligned with those of the early literacy component of the ELORS, and although theoretical and social validity has been demonstrated, further examination of reliability and validity is needed (Gillis, West, Coleman, 2010b).

Case Example

As Sherman Academy learns about the process of universal screening and becomes familiar with the early literacy and math screening tools, the staff decide they would like to incorporate universal screening of early academic skills into their current assessment plan. Together, the team develops a school-wide screening plan, selects screening measures, and schedules trainings in preparation for conducting universal screening of early academic skills during the upcoming fall.

Summary

Given the relationship of preschool academic performance to later academic success, it is imperative that schools have sufficient academic supports in place for young children. One way to identify children who may need additional supports and to inform selection of developmentally appropriate academic interventions is through universal screening. This chapter provided an introduction to the universal screening process and its application in preschool settings. Following the introduction, a brief review of instruments developed specifically for use in screening and monitoring the early literacy and math skills of preschool children was presented. Although the development of universal screening instruments designed specifically for preschool children is still in its infancy, tools are available, and this area of research and practice continues to grow. As such, it is important for educators to not only be aware of universal screening tools and stay abreast of the continued research in this area, but also be cognizant of the differences in tools and careful in their selection. For example, educators may wish to consider the factors such as technical properties, age, cultural and linguistic fit, range of assessed skills, availability of progress monitoring tools, family involvement, materials (e.g., technology), and availability of specific screening instruments.

4

Academic Interventions and Progress Monitoring

Tiers 1, 2, and 3

In working with their educational consultant, Sherman Academy established a plan to begin screening all students' early literacy and math skills during the upcoming fall. In preparation, Sherman staff members also wanted to learn about using screening data to inform their selection of tiered instruction and interventions. They wished in addition to learn ways to monitor their students' progress once appropriate interventions were in place. Together, Sherman Academy and their educational consultant began outlining options for intervention and progress monitoring.

Universal screening was introduced in Chapter 3 as one of the cornerstones of multitiered service delivery models. Additional cornerstones include effective instruction, evidence-based interventions, and progress monitoring across multiple tiers (Burns & Gibbons, 2012). Many models of MTSS structure service delivery across three tiers. Within Tier 1, effective instruction and evidence-based interventions are delivered to all students, class-wide or in small groups. Students who may be at-risk of learning difficulties or who do not respond to Tier 1 supports also receive Tier 2 supports—intensive instruction or intervention often in small-group settings. Finally, the few students who need further support receive Tier 3 supports in the form of individualized interventions. Across all tiers, student progress is monitored to measure response to instruction and intervention. This chapter begins with an overview of these components, followed by *examples* of select early literacy and early math *programs* or *strategies* for each tier, and concludes with a discussion of how these components have been applied in early childhood settings.

Tier Overview

Tier 1. Within a MTSS, Tier 1 supports are delivered through quality instruction provided to all children, typically through delivery of a core curriculum and evidence-based interventions. In early childhood education settings, this translates to a core curriculum coupled with intentional teaching, with the expectation that 70 to 80% of children will meet standards, as demonstrated in the universal screening data (Buysse & Peisner-Feinberg, 2010).

Selecting a core curriculum that effectively meets the learning needs of all students can be challenging, given that there are many curricula from which to choose, and there is not a general consensus about which are most effective (National Center for Education Research, 2008). Nevertheless, three guiding principles can assist in the selection of a core curriculum. First, early childhood education settings must examine the evidence demonstrating effectiveness of the various curricula in meeting the learning goals of the school. For example, a preschool composed primarily of Latino dual language learners might begin by examining the research to determine which curricula have been shown to be effective in meeting the learning needs of this population. During this selection process, educators must also determine the extent to which available curricula are developmentally appropriate for the children receiving instruction. Finally, educators must also examine the degree to which available curricula address all learning domains. For example, curricula focusing on language and early literacy are certainly useful in promoting language and literacy development in young children and could be used as supplementary curricula. However, a core curriculum will be comprehensive in nature and address all learning domains, including early literacy and early math, for example.

Coupled with a strong core curriculum, intentional teaching of all young learners is another essential component of Tier 1 supports in early childhood education settings. "Intentional teaching occurs through the purposeful organization of the classroom environment and the provision of planned, developmentally appropriate activities to offer opportunities for children to learn and develop important skills" (Buysse & Peisner-Feinberg, 2010, p. 7). Intentional teaching occurs in congruence with the core curriculum and may also occur in the provision of supplemental class-wide or small-group interventions available to all learners. The progress of children receiving Tier 1 supports (all children) via a strong core curriculum and intentional teaching is periodically monitored through universal screening, as described in Chapter 3.

Tier 2.   Young children who do not respond positively to the core curriculum and class-wide or small-group interventions continue receiving Tier 1 supports, along with the Tier 2 supports of targeted interventions within small groups and embedded learning activities (Buysse & Peisner-Feinberg, 2010). Generally, 15 to 25% of children are in need of Tier 2 supports, and the supports emphasize discrete academic skills that contribute to overall learning. As compared to Tier 1, these added supports are only provided for children whose performance on the universal screening measures does not meet classroom, school, or district academic standards, and small groups are created around children with similar needs. For example, if upon administering the IGDIs as a universal screener of early literacy skills, Sherman Academy found a subset of students whose performance on Picture Naming was below expected levels, these children might then be grouped together to receive additional, focused instruction on skills related to expressive language development. Similarly, if student performance on the Pre-kindergarten Early Numeracy Screener showed subsets of students struggling with number selection and number naming skills, small groups structured around those learning goals would be created.

Unlike the comprehensive core curriculum, the curricula selected for use in Tier 2 small groups are domain-specific to directly address the learning needs of the children in groups of three to six children. With young children, delivery of this instruction is sequential and explicit while in the groups and might occur approximately 15 minutes per day. As well, to enhance the knowledge acquired through instruction and provide additional learning opportunities, learning activities linked to small-group instruction are embedded in the class activities. The progress of children receiving Tier 2 supports is monitored more frequently than most children and usually occurs every 2 to 3 weeks with the same, or similar, measures used for universal screening. Ultimately, small-group instruction will be discontinued for children whose academic performance improves and the improvement is maintained over time.

Tier 3. For the few children who do not respond as anticipated to Tier 1 and Tier 2 supports (approximately 5%), additional Tier 3 supports are offered. Tier 3 supports typically include individualized and intensive interventions that may involve scaffolding strategies and are provided for these children along with Tier 1 and Tier 2 supports (Buysse & Peisner-Feinberg, 2010). As compared to Tier 1 and Tier 2 supports, Tier 3 interventions are selected for, and tailored specifically to, the needs of an individual child. At Tier 3, research-based interventions (e.g., an intervention designed to promote phonemic awareness) are combined with more directive teaching strategies and delivered to a child one-on-one. Progress monitoring for children receiving Tier 3 services occurs at least weekly.

Together, these three tiers (and sometimes more, depending on the specific model) provide a framework for ensuring that supports are in place to facilitate learning for all children. Furthermore, aligning progress monitoring practices with the intensity of supports (e.g., children who receive Tier 3 supports are assessed more often than children who receive only Tier 1 or Tier 1 and 2 supports together) ensures each child's supports will be adapted to continue meeting his or her learning needs. Below, *examples* of early childhood curricula and interventions appropriate for each of the three tiers are presented. These examples are a combination of widespread, effective, and promising practices in early childhood education.

Tier 1 Preschool Core Curricula

The Creative Curriculum System for Preschool. The Creative Curriculum System for Preschool (Dodge, Colker, & Heroman, 2010) is a comprehensive, research-based curriculum commonly used in early childhood education settings. Aligned with Head Start Child Development, Early Learning Framework, and state early learning standards, the Creative Curriculum addresses the academic and social-emotional needs of young children (birth through kindergarten) with and without disabilities and is available in English and Spanish. Materials to support the needs of dual language learners, as well as an assessment system for all learners (Teaching Strategies, 2010a; GOLD Assessment System) are also included in the curriculum.

The Creative Curriculum is guided by the following five principles: positive interactions and relationships with adults provide a critical foundation for successful learning; social–emotional competence is a significant factor in school success; constructive, purposeful play supports essential learning;

the physical environment affects the type and quality of learning interactions; and teacher–family partnerships promote development and learning (Teaching Strategies, 2010b). Based on these principles, the program is organized around curriculum, embedded assessment, professional development, and family connection, and is presented as a series of studies throughout the school year (e.g., Do all balls bounce?). Through these studies, growth in the following areas of development and learning is promoted: social-emotional, physical, language, cognitive, literacy, mathematics, science and technology, social studies, the arts, and English-language acquisition. Resources such as teaching guides and intentional teaching cards provide support to teachers in the classroom. Additional information about the Creative Curriculum System for Preschool can be found at the Teaching Strategies website (www. teachingstrategies.com).

DLM Early Childhood Express. The DLM Early Childhood Express (2011) is another comprehensive preschool curriculum designed to meet the literacy, fine arts, science, personal development, technology, math, social studies, health and safety, and physical development needs of young children. As well, materials are available in English and Spanish, and the lessons provide support to the teacher in working with dual language learners. The DLM Early Childhood Express is composed of eight themes introduced every 4 weeks. Each new unit is developed around a question such as, "How do living things grow and change?" and learning opportunities to promote the development of the aforementioned learning goals are integrated into each unit, as are assessments and opportunities for home–school collaboration. Instructional activities are provided to the whole class via circle time and in small groups during center time. Furthermore, the curriculum includes online resources to support teaching and learning. Additional information about the DLM Early Childhood Express curriculum can be found at the McGraw-Hill Education website (www.mheonline.com).

Tier 2 Academic Interventions in Preschool

Early Literacy. The Center for Response to Intervention in Early Childhood (CRTIEC) is a collaborative effort between professionals of the Juniper Gardens Children's Project (University of Kansas), Schoenbaum Family Center at Weinland Park (The Ohio State University), Center for Early Education and Development (University of Minnesota), and Dynamic Measurement

Group (DMG) in Eugene, Oregon (Center for Response to Intervention in Early Childhood, 2012). As noted in Chapter 1, one of the many notable endeavors is the advancement of Tier 2 and Tier 3 (see below) language and early literacy interventions. For example, the center is further developing the use of skill-focused listening centers (SFLCs) as a Tier 2 support (Goldstein & Kaminski, 2010). Through the use of SFLCs, small groups of children individually listen to audio recordings of instructional lessons while following along in a book designed for the particular lesson and responding to visual and audio prompts. These centers work toward closing gaps from Tier 1 instruction by promoting skill-building in phonological awareness, print awareness/alphabet knowledge, vocabulary, and comprehension, and student progress is assessed each week. This SFLC format is quite innovative in that it increases the child's exposure to instructional material and opportunities to respond, while also enhancing opportunities to learn given limited classroom personnel.

Early Math. As noted in Chapter 3, universal screening practices for reading are more fully developed than those for math, and math screening practices are more fully developed than those for writing at the elementary level. MTSS academic intervention practices at the elementary level are similar, as reading interventions are fairly well established, and effectiveness studies of math interventions are emerging. As might be expected, then, the development of Tier 2 and Tier 3 math interventions for young children in early childhood education settings is in its infancy, as much attention is paid first to developing language and literacy skills. Nevertheless, melding what is known about best practices for math instruction with young children with the level of support needed for children receiving Tier 2 services, a general framework for Tier 2 interventions can be developed.

General instructional practices for teaching math to young children include the provision of explicit, sequenced, scaffolded, and differentiated instruction, as well as opportunities to practice newly acquired knowledge and skills. Given that children in need of Tier 2 supports require supplementary instruction of discrete math skills and can be grouped with other children who have similar math needs, early childhood educators may use these practices in the context of small groups to promote the acquisition of basic math skills (e.g., counting) and structured classroom activities (e.g., focused math learning centers and integrated learning centers) to facilitate opportunities for practice and corrective feedback.

Pre-K Mathematics. In addition, certain curricula, such as Pre-K Mathematics (Klein, Starkey, & Ramirez, 2002), have shown promise when combined with a comprehensive core curriculum and may be suitable for use as a Tier 2 support to supplement the Tier 1 core curriculum. Pre-K Mathematics is a curriculum including seven themes and is designed to cover number sense and enumeration, arithmetic reasoning (fall), spatial sense and geometric reasoning, pattern sense and pattern construction, arithmetic reasoning (spring), measurement and data representation, and logical relations throughout the school year. Instruction is delivered in small groups of four to six children across the school year, and opportunities for home involvement are offered every week or two with materials that are available in English and Spanish. Guidance for differentiated instruction to meet the needs of all children is also provided. Though the Pre-K Mathematics curriculum has shown positive effects with young children, interested educators can also obtain guidelines for selecting and implementing early childhood math curricula from a joint position statement developed by the National Association for the Education of Young Children (NAEYC) and the National Council of Teachers of Mathematics (NCTM) (National Association for the Education of Young Children and National Council of Teachers of Mathematics, 2002).

Tier 3 Academic Interventions in Preschool

Early Literacy. CRTIEC is also advancing knowledge of Tier 3 language and early literacy interventions. Because Tier 3 supports are tailored to the needs of children who do not meet standards with the provision of Tier 1 and Tier 3 supports, the Tier 3 interventions posited by CRTIEC are intensive, skill-directed, and administered individually or in very small groups by a trained interventionist. Instruction is explicit and sequenced and typically focused on a particular domain, such as phonological awareness. For example, as presented by Greenwood et al. (2011), interventions in phonological awareness would follow this sequence: "(a) letter naming game; (b) introduction/review of target skill; (c) guided practice of target skill in early literacy game; and (d) contextualization of target skill in song, poem, or finger play" (p. 9). CRTIEC's Tier 3 interventions are provided three times per week, for 5 to 10 minutes. Additional information about CRTIEC's advancement of Tier 2 and Tier 3 language and early literacy interventions can be found on their website (http://www.crtiec.org/interventionsfortier2and3/index.shtml).

Additional Considerations Regarding Tiered Academic
Interventions in Preschools

Although these tiers do provide a general framework for MTSS within early childhood education settings, barriers (or additional considerations) do exist (Greenwood et al., 2011). As Greenwood et al. (2011) note, these challenges include workforce quality, lack of knowledge and resources, lack of evidence-based curricula, lack of guidance regarding the incorporation of evidence-based intervention strategies for Tiers 2 and 3 into classroom instruction, and availability of administrative support and resources. In this chapter, we will focus on the lack of evidence-based curricula and guidance in the incorporation of intervention strategies for Tiers 2 and 3.

Evidence-Based Curricula. Reviews of preschool curricula· can be found through the Preschool Evaluation Curriculum Research (PECR) initiative (initiated by the Institute of Education Sciences, 2012; National Center for Education Research, 2008) as well as the What Works Clearinghouse (WWC; Institute of Education Sciences, 2012). Through an experimental design, 12 PECR research teams implemented the following 14 curricula with preschool children and followed them through kindergarten:

Bright Beginnings
Creative Curriculum (implemented by research teams from Vanderbilt
    University and the University of North Carolina at Charlotte):
Creative Curriculum with Ladders to Literacy
Curiosity Corner
DLM Early Childhood Express supplemented with *Open Court Reading Pre-K*
Doors to Discovery
Early Literacy and Learning Model (ELLM)
Language-Focused Curriculum
Let's Begin with the Letter People
Literacy Express
Pre-K Mathematics supplemented with *DLM Early Childhood Express*
    Math Software Project Approach
Project Construct
Ready, Set, Leap!

RTI International and Mathematica Policy Research evaluated the efficacy of the curricula and found that two curricula had positive impacts on children's learning outcomes in prekindergarten: *DLM Early Childhood Express* supplemented with *Open Court Reading Pre-K* (reading, phonological awareness, and language) and *Pre-K Mathematics* supplemented with *DLM Early Childhood Express Math software* (mathematics). *DLM Early Childhood Express* supplemented with *Open Court Reading Pre-K*, along with three other curricula, also had a positive impact during kindergarten. In addition to having a positive impact on the children's learning outcomes, the following eight curricula demonstrated a positive impact on classroom outcomes:

Bright Beginnings (early literacy instruction and phonological awareness instruction)

Creative Curriculum (University of North Carolina at Charlotte; classroom quality, teacher–child interaction, early literacy instruction, and early language instruction)

Creative Curriculum with Ladders to Literacy (early literacy instruction)

Curiosity Corner (early language instruction)

DLM Early Childhood Express supplemented with *Open Court Reading Pre-K* (phonological awareness instruction)

Doors to Discovery (early literacy instruction and early language instruction)

Let's Begin with the Letter People (classroom quality and early literacy instruction)

Literacy Express (classroom quality and phonological awareness instruction)

Findings from the WWC showed positive effects for two early literacy curricula (*Daisy Quest* and *Literacy Express*) and two early math curricula (*Building Blocks for Math* [*SRA Real Math*] and *Pre-K Mathematics*]. Though the PECR and WWC findings are certainly promising, they also highlight the true lack of evidence-based curricula.

Evidence-Based Intervention Strategies for Tiers 2 and 3. Similar to the evidence base for core curricula in early childhood education, there is research support for some Tier 2 and Tier 3 intervention strategies. That is, specific interventions that address discrete academic skills and can be used to support the core curriculum, either through small-group or one-on-one service delivery, have been, and continue to be, implemented and evaluated with young children. However, research evaluating the effectiveness of such intervention is still emerging. Furthermore, these studies often occur in controlled settings or instruction is delivered by researchers, rather than general classroom educators. As such, little guidance and support exists for educators to actually incorporate evidence-based intervention strategies for Tiers 2 and 3 into their classroom routine (Greenwood et al., 2011). Future research may examine ways to demonstrate intervention feasibility, acceptability, and effectiveness within MTSS models implemented in existing classroom environments. Despite such obstacles, however, some early childhood education settings are taking steps to implement MTSS models to meet children's learning goals. This chapter concludes with a description of some of these efforts.

Tiered Academic Interventions in Practice

As introduced in chapter 1, models of MTSS in early childhood education settings are in various stages of implementation and evaluation across multiple sites in the United States. Below, academic intervention and progress monitoring practices used in The Literacy Partnership, Recognition and Response, and others are presented.

The Literacy Partnership. The Literacy Partnership was a 3-year collaborative effort between three charter schools in Washington, DC; the University of Maryland Hearing and Speech Sciences Department of College Park, Maryland; Educational Solutions, LLC of Arlington, Virginia; and The Chesapeake Center of Springfield, Virginia (Literacy Partnership, 2007). Together, this partnership developed and implemented a plan to address oral language, phonological awareness, print awareness, alphabet knowledge, and cognitive development of children across three tiers in early education settings. In Tier 1, the partnership facilitated implementation and evaluation of the Creative Curriculum Literacy Component-Preschool, along with Instructional Supplements (developed by Educational Solutions, LLC), to provide class-wide instruction for all children. Instructional Supplements consisted of complementary literacy activities, designed for small-group and individual service delivery, and meant to support at-risk students. Children receiving Tier 2 intervention received instruction in small groups or individually via Promoting Awareness in Speech Sounds (PASS), as well as Receptive and Expressive Approach to Language and Learning (REALL), from speech language pathologists to supplement their receipt of Tier 1 instruction. PASS provides supplementary instruction in phonological awareness, and REALL provides supplementary instruction in vocabulary enhancement. All supports are aligned with the Creative Curriculum Literacy Component. Finally, children in need of additional Tier 3 supports received intensive instruction from literacy mentors or speech language pathologists. Child outcomes were monitored via the IGDIs. Information about work of The Literacy Partnership, as well as early literacy resources for teachers and parents, can be found on their website (http://literacypartnershiperfgrant.com/Resources.html).

Recognition and Response (R&R). R&R is a MTSS model developed for use in early childhood education settings (FPG Child Development Institute, 2012). Developed by University of North Carolina-Chapel Hill researchers at the Frank Porter Graham Child Development Institute and implemented with ethnically and linguistically diverse children in community childcare programs, Head Start programs, and public preschools, this model focuses on the language, literacy, and math needs of young children 3 to 5 years of age and has been studied with Latino dual language learners. Research designed to further develop and evaluate the language and literacy system is underway. Similarly, a study that is designed to develop and evaluate an R&R math system based on research supporting the language and literacy system, is also underway.

During its first implementation study, the language and literacy system of R&R was implemented with over 300 children 4 years of age in over 20 early childhood education settings in Maryland and Florida. All sites selected for the implementation study were already implementing a comprehensive core curriculum. Following universal screening, teachers selected four children from each classroom to receive Tier 2 supports in small-group instructional settings for 15 minutes per day across 2 months. Via the Read It Again—PreK! curriculum, children received instruction in vocabulary and comprehension, sound awareness, print knowledge, and alphabet knowledge. Children in need of Tier 3 supports received individualized scaffolding in addition to small-group instruction. The vocabulary, letter naming, and phonological awareness skills of children receiving Tier 2 and Tier 3 supports were monitored with the mCLASS: CIRCLE early literacy assessment system, an earlier version of the mCLASS+ system. Additional information about how R&R is being used to meet the language, literacy, and math needs of young children can be found at its website (http://randr.fpg.unc.edu/).

Prairie Children Preschool. Prairie Children Preschool is a community preschool of the Indian Prairie School District #204 in Aurora, Illinois (Young,

Snow, Frech, & Shields, 2011). Established in 1998, the school consists of 21 classrooms with approximately 16 children per class, is located within the district's early childhood education facility, and is attended by approximately 500 children 3 to 5 years of age. For Tier 1, the school has adopted The Creative Curriculum for Preschool because it is aligned with the Illinois Early Learning Standards, along with PBIS and the Promoting Alternative Thinking Strategies (PATHS) program (Domitrovich, Greenberg, Kusche, & Cortes, 2004). Children receive additional supports at Tiers 2 and 3, and their outcomes are monitored with the Teaching Strategies GOLD Assessment System (Teaching Strategies, 2010a).

State Initiatives. In addition to the aforementioned MTSS models, several states have developed guidelines or manuals to guide the adoption of tiered service delivery in early childhood education settings. For example, Kansas has developed a comprehensive MTSS framework designed to guide the delivery of evidence-based, system-wide practices to promote students' reading, math, and behavioral well-being (Kansas MTSS, 2008). The Kansas Multi-Tier System of Supports website offers extensive resources and implementation guides addressing the needs of children from early childhood through graduation. Similarly, as described in Chapter 1, Colorado has also adopted a MTSS, Colorado's Pre-K RTI model (National Center for Learning Disabilities, 2009). Aligned with the state's core principles, the Pre-K RTI model is being implemented in at least 10 to 15 districts and is in an early developmental phase in approximately 20 to 30 districts.

Summary

Meeting the academic needs of diverse learners is not a new concept for early childhood education. However, formally framing a continuum of academic service delivery around tiers and providing a structure for ongoing assessment offers the opportunity for the field to expand and improve upon already effective instructional practices. MTSS models of academic interventions also provide the field with an opportunity to identify areas for growth, such as the provision of math supports across tiers.

5

Universal Screening of Social-Emotional and Behavioral Functioning

Mental health is "a state of well-being in which every individual realizes his or her own potential, can cope with the normal stresses of life, can work productively and fruitfully, and is able to make a contribution to her or his community" (World Health Organization, 2012). According to the U.S. Surgeon General's report, 20% of children and adolescents have a mental health problem (U.S. Department of Health and Human Services, 1999). Unfortunately, similar prevalence rates also exist for the early childhood population with epidemiologists reporting a mean occurrence rate of 19.5% (Egger & Angold, 2006). It is even possible that the above percentages are underestimates. The prevalence rates only included those children and adolescents who had been identified as having problems, not those with disorders who remain unidentified and without treatment, and not those with subclinical symptoms who are at-risk for the development of a problem (Feeney-Kettler & Kratochwill, 2008).

For children who may be at-risk for social-emotional and behavioral problems, early childhood professionals can play a critical role in screening for risk status, in identifying problems, and in providing or referring children for evidence-based, preventive interventions. This chapter provides an overview of the importance of social-emotional and behavioral screening in early childhood as a method of promoting mental health. It also includes key considerations for early childhood professionals before the selection of a screening tool, as well as a table of available social-emotional and behavioral screeners. A case example is provided at the conclusion of the chapter, along with resources for early childhood social-emotional and behavioral development and screening.

Why Screen for Social-Emotional and Behavioral Problems?

Screening for social-emotional and behavioral problems involves the early detection of symptoms before the symptoms worsen and develop into disorder(s). Screening is a method linked to prevention. By screening all young children for their social-emotional and behavioral health, children with beginning symptoms of problems can be referred for evidence-based, preventive interventions before their problems become worse and interfere with their development (Feeney-Kettler, Kratochwill, & Kettler, 2012).

Consequences of Untreated Social-Emotional and Behavioral Problems. Unidentified and untreated social-emotional and behavioral problems are extremely problematic. Not only do the symptoms of problems impact the individual with the problem, but they also affect the family, the school, and society as a whole. For example, the child with the problem experiences the symptoms (e.g., intense anxiety that interferes with social, emotional, and academic functioning); the family tries to cope with the child's behavioral manifestations of the problem (e.g., intense meltdowns many times every day); the school is accountable to teach the child academic skills despite social-emotional and behavioral problems (e.g., symptoms of the problem are interfering with the child's ability to learn and may also be disruptive to the rest of the students in the classroom); and society bears the cost of the problems (e.g., caregiver time off from work to cope with the child's problems, academic failure that results in school dropout, the child's potential development of additional problems that require many more treatment resources compared to the original problem).

In summary, untreated social-emotional and behavioral problems yield difficulties both in the present and in the future. Present difficulties refer to symptom impairment (e.g., difficulty concentrating, trouble making friends, difficulty participating in school activities) and the negative impact of the symptoms on the child's overall development (e.g., lack of social relationships); future difficulties encompass the long-term consequences of symptom impairment, such as school dropout, the development of secondary problems, and adults who are less able to function successfully in society. A more proactive model of service delivery, that involves early detection through screening, and then evidence-based preventive intervention, will likely be much more effective and less costly than historical, reactive "wait to fail" models.

Origins of Social-Emotional and Behavioral Problems. Developmental psycho-pathologists have found that many disorders begin in the early childhood period (National Scientific Council on the Developing Child, 2008). Parents have also reported that older children with disorders evidenced signs of problems during early childhood, even though their children did not receive intervention until late elementary school (Kenny, Oliver, & Poppe, 2002). This information, coupled with the consequences of untreated social-emotional and behavioral problems, highlights the importance of screening for social-emotional and behavioral functioning during the early childhood years, and provides a rationale for the early childhood professionals to actively screen young children for their social-emotional and behavioral health.

Key Considerations before Selecting a Screening Tool

Key Questions. Even before early childhood professionals think about selecting a screening tool, it is imperative to consider the questions presented by Feeney-Kettler, Kratochwill, Kaiser, Hemmeter, and Kettler (2010). These questions have been adapted into the *Social-Emotional and Behavioral Screening: Pre-Planning Questionnaire* (see the *Early Childhood Education* companion website).

First, the *population of interest* must be determined. Early childhood professionals must identify the age of the group or individual(s) they want to screen. For example, there are different screeners available for 3-year-old children than there are for 5-year-old children.

Second, the *type of social-emotional and behavioral problem* for which one wants to screen must be identified. Generally, when screening for social-emotional and behavioral problems, screening is implemented more broadly, examining the risk status for internalizing and externalizing problems in general. Internalizing symptoms refer to behaviors and emotions that a child directs inward, toward him- or herself; they are not often directly observable, which may make them difficult to identify (Feeney-Kettler, Kratochill, & Kettler, 2009; Feil, Severson, & Walker, 1998). Examples may include acting worried or nervous, seeming shy, manifesting low energy, and sleeping too much or too little (Feeney-Kettler, Kratochwill, & Kettler, 2009). External-izing problems refer to behaviors that a child directs outward, toward others and the environment; they are directly observable, making them easier to identify than internalizing problems (Feeney-Kettler, Kratochwill, & Ket-tler, 2012; Feil et al., 1998) Examples may include destroying toys or prop-erty, harming people or animals, arguing, disobeying rules, and fighting (see Feeney-Kettler, Kratochwill, & Kettler, 2009).

It is very important to remember that all young children may experience some internalizing or externalizing symptoms at some point during their maturation. It is the frequency, intensity, and duration of the symptoms that should be noted. Additionally, when these symptoms begin to impact the child and those around the child, cause for concern may be warranted.

Third, the *method of screening* must be determined. Screening of social-emotional and behavioral problems can be accomplished by screening every child, by screening a small group of children, or by screening individual target children only. Rating scales or questionnaires may be the method of choice. Alternatively, a tiered approach that involves multiple stages of screen-ing may be preferable, whereby children identified as at risk on a screener implemented to the entire school or class receive additional screening dur-ing a second screening stage, and potentially further assessment if risk status continues during a third screening stage (Feeney-Kettler, Kratochwill, Kaiser, et al., 2010; Walker, Severson, & Feil, 1995). Multiple stage screening meth-ods are designed to be cost- and time-efficient for use with large numbers of children; if they function ideally, then only a small number of students will need to be screened during the second screening stage, followed by an even smaller number during the third screening stage (Feil et al., 1998; Walker et al., 1995). In this multiple stage model, children might be nominated by teachers for severity of internalizing or externalizing symptoms in the first screening stage. Children at-risk based on teacher nomination may then be screened further by having teachers complete behavior rating scales during the second screening stage. Children still at-risk during the second screening stage may then be observed or a parent/child interview may be conducted during a third assessment stage. If screening a large group such as an entire classroom or school, a multiple-stage screener may be more preferable than using a rating scale that takes 15 to 20 minutes to complete per individual child.

The format method of screening also refers to the type of screener that is desirable. This involves considering the response format (e.g., circling *never, sometimes,* or *often* in response to descriptions of behavior on a rating scale;

providing qualitative answers to written questions) and the administration format (e.g., interview, completion of rating scale or questionnaire independently) of the screener.

Fourth, the *type of informant* must be chosen. Informant refers to the individual who will provide information about the child's social-emotional and behavioral functioning, and may include biological parents, foster parents, guardians, teachers, childcare providers, or other individuals who know the child well. When screening young children for their social-emotional and behavioral health, it is recommended that multiple informants be used, such as all primary caregivers (Feeney-Kettler, Kratochwill, & Kettler, 2012; Levitt, Saka, Hunter Romanelli, & Hoagwood, 2007). Some problematic behaviors may be setting-specific and may only be observable in one setting (Feeney-Kettler, Kratochwill, & Kettler, 2012). A child who is always irritable at school may not be irritable at home, or a child who has many meltdowns at home, may not have meltdowns at school. "Reliance on one informant, who only observes the child in one setting does not address the whole child" and may present "partial information with regard to the child's" social-emotional and behavioral functioning (Feeney-Kettler, Kratochwill, & Kettler, 2012, p. 199). Therefore, if an early childhood setting has the resources, best practices in screening young children would recommend including informants from both the school and home settings.

Once these four preliminary questions are answered, the infrastructure for screening implementation needs examination.

Infrastructure for Screening Implementation: Required Resources. Screening for social-emotional and behavioral problems requires a plan that involves a variety of resources that have been adapted into the *Social-Emotional and Behavioral Screening: Pre-Planning—Infrastructure and Resources Questionnaire* (see the *Early Childhood Education* companion website). It is important for early childhood professionals to carefully examine the infrastructure in place to determine the level of resources available for implementing a screener (Glover & Albers, 2007). Infrastructure refers to the personnel necessary for both planning and implementing the screening process. Personnel resources involve designated individuals for the following areas (see Feeney-Kettler, Kratochwill, Kaiser, et al., 2010):

- Providing professional development in screener administration, scoring, and communication of results

- Administering the screener
- Who will administer the screener?
- When will the screener be administered?
- Scoring the screener
- Who will score the screener?
- Is scoring by hand or does it require computer software?
- What type of scores are used (e.g., raw scores, T-scores)
- Who will interpret the results of the scores?
- Delivering feedback, especially to those families of children identified at "at-risk" for the development of a problem, and
- Providing evidence-based preventive interventions or having referral agencies available to meet the needs of children identified as being "at-risk."

Financial resources must also be examined. These resources involve the monies necessary (a) to purchase the screener, the manual, and related scoring software; (b) to provide the aforementioned professional development, screener administration, scoring, and feedback to families; and (c) to provide evidence-based preventive interventions when necessary.

Early childhood professionals must examine the level of resources their program has available so that they can determine the nature and scope of their screening program. If resources are limited, a screener that costs less money to purchase and score, that can be used with minimal training, and that can be photocopied for multiple uses may be more advisable. A partnership with the local school district for screening, further assessment, and evidence-based preventative interventions for children identified as "at-risk," may be an avenue for exploration.

Additional Evaluation Criteria. Glover and Albers (2007) provide additional suggestions for considering and evaluating screeners. Some important factors to note are whether or not screener implementation is feasible; whether the screener is acceptable to key stakeholders, such as parents, teachers, and administrators; whether accommodations exist for those who may have difficulty completing the screener (e.g., oral administration for those who cannot read); and whether the screener's results can provide information relevant to determining appropriate preventive interventions.

Psychometric Properties. The final step before selecting a screening instrument is to be knowledgeable about psychometric properties. This means that early childhood professionals need to examine the reliability of scores as well as the inferences that can be made based on the validity of the scores. There are various types of reliability and validity, which are beyond the scope of this chapter to review. Early childhood professionals are referred to Kettler and Feeney-Kettler (2011) for a review of psychometric properties for a screening instrument. Of particular importance are conditional probability indices (sensitivity, specificity, positive predictive value and negative predictive value), all of which illustrate how well the screening system accurately distinguishes children with problems from children without problems. *Sensitivity* is the likelihood that a child who has or is at-risk for a social-emotional or behavioral problem will be correctly identified as having a problem; *specificity* is the likelihood that a child who does not have or is not at-risk for a social-emotional or behavioral problem will be correctly identified as not having a problem; *positive predictive value* is the likelihood that a child identified as at-risk or with a problem actually has a problem; and *negative predictive value* is the likelihood that a student not identified as at-risk or with a problem actually does not have a problem (Kettler & Feeny-Kettler, 2011).

Related to how well the conditional probability indices are functioning are the terms *false positive* and *false negative*. If a screener incorrectly identifies children with problems, when the children do not have problems, then this will result in an increased false positive rate. A high number of false positives may mean an increase in prevention programming and further assessment resources being spent on children who do not require these resources (Levitt et al., 2007), as well as unnecessary stress for families of incorrectly identified children (Feeney-Kettler, Kratochwill, & Kettler, 2012). On the other hand, a high number of false negatives (not identifying children with problems or at-risk for problems when they actually have problems) may mean an increase in the number of children who remain unidentified and without intervention (Feeney-Kettler, Kratochwill, & Kettler, 2012).

In general, high conditional probability index values are preferred (greater than or equal to .80; Kettler & Feeney-Kettler, 2011). Unfortunately, most screeners do not meet this criterion across all index values (see Levitt et al., 2007). Kettler and Feeney-Kettler (2011) provide a discussion of the ranges of conditional probability index values and the potential conditions for each value to be acceptable. For example, values below .40 are considered *very low*. Values between .40 and .59 are *low*, and values between .60 and .80 are considered *moderate*. Depending on the purpose of the screener and its environment, different ranges may be acceptable for the various indices. For example, when using a multiple stage screener, Levitt et al. (2007) state that high negative predictive power and high sensitivity are important for the first phase of a screening system so that children who need to be identified will actually be identified as "at-risk." The later screening stages (i.e., stage 2 and 3) need to be more specific and to have greater positive predictive values (Kettler & Feeney-Kettler, 2011; Levitt et al., 2007).

A Special Note on Screening Children from Culturally and Linguistically Diverse Backgrounds. When evaluating whether or not a screener is appropriate for a specific population, it is important to examine the screener's manual to see the demographic characteristics (age, race, gender, primary langue, state of residence, etc.) of the instrument's normative population. The term *normative population* refers to the sample of children to whom the screener was administered, whose scores, based on those of same-age peers, are used to show what is average or typical development for a group (Sattler, 2008). For instance, if the screener's normative population was a homogeneous group of 3-year-old children who were White, then the normative data may not be generalizable to a population of 3-year-old children who are Latino or Latina. Additionally, although some screeners may be available in other languages, such as Spanish, it may be the case that the psychometric properties reported in the instrument's manual are *not* for the translated screener (Feeney-Kettler, Kratochwill, Kaiser, et al., 2010). There may be separate normative data for translated screeners, and this data may be based on sample sizes much smaller than the sample size used to derive the normative data for the English version of the screener (Feeney-Kettler, Kratochwill, Kaiser, et al., 2010). Translated versions of screeners should be held to the same psychometric standards as the English versions of screeners.

Additionally, some behaviors may be acceptable and considered appropriate in some cultures, and not acceptable or appropriate in other cultures. This highlights the importance of incorporating multiple informants, as discussed above, when screening young children for their social-emotional and behavioral functioning. Some screeners (Ages and Stages Questionnaire-Social Emotional [ASQ-SE]; Squires, Bricker, & Twombly, 2002) actually allow for the elimination of certain items that may not be culturally or ethnically appropriate (Feeney-Kettler, Kratchowill, Kaiser, et al., 2010).

Examples of Screening Systems

There are a limited number of instruments available for screening young children for social-emotional and behavioral problems (Feeney-Kettler, Kratochwill, & Kettler, 2011). Feeney-Kettler, Kratochwill, Kaiser, et al. (2010) conducted a review of measures designed to assess the social and emotional functioning of children between the ages of 3 and 5 years. The authors identified three published measures and one unpublished measure that met their literature search criteria. Criteria included the age of the population (3 to 5 years old) and broad-band measures of overall social and emotional development, rather than ore narrow-band areas (e.g., adaptive behavior or pervasive developmental disorders). Criteria also included whether the measures were cost and time efficient to be administered to a large volume of students for universal screening, rather than more time intensive, comprehensive assessment measures, like the *Behavior Assessment System for Children* (Reynolds & Kampaus, 2004). The three published measures included the Early Screening Project (ESP; Walker et al., 1995), the *Behavior and Emotional Screening System* (BASC-2 BESS; Kamphaus & Reynolds, 2007), and the *Ages and Stages Questionnaires: Social-Emotional* (ASQ-SE; Squires et al., 2002); the *Preschool Behavior Screening System* (PBSS; Feeney-Kettler, Kratochwill, & Kettler, 2011) was unpublished. (For an in-depth discussion of each of these screening instruments and their psychometric properties, readers are referred to Feeney-Kettler, Kratochwill, Kaiser, et al., 2010).

It is important to note that the ESP is the only published multiple stage screening system for the early childhood population. The first screening stage involves teacher nomination of five classroom children based on internalizing and externalizing symptoms, and a rank ordering of children based on the severity of symptoms. The three highest ranked children with internalizing symptoms and the three highest ranked children with externalizing symptoms advance for additional screening. The second screening stage involves teacher completion of (a) a questionnaire indicating the presence or absence of critical behaviors, (b) a questionnaire rating the frequency of adaptive and maladaptive behaviors, (c) a questionnaire rating the frequency of aggressive behaviors (completed on highest ranked externalizing children only), and (d) a questionnaire rating the frequency of social behavior (completed on the highest ranked internalizing children only). For children at-risk during the second screening stage, a third stage involving observations of students is optional.

Although currently unpublished, the PBSS is also a multiple stage screener. Unlike the ESP, the PBSS incorporates parents throughout the entire screening process, involving multiple informants (Feeney-Kettler, Kratochwill, & Kettler, 2012). The PBSS also allows for as many children as necessary within a classroom who may be at risk for the development of social-emotional and behavioral problems to receive further screening during the second stage. Recall that the ESP only allows for the top three children with internalizing symptoms and for the top three children with externalizing symptoms to receive further screening during a second screening stage. With the PBSS, teachers rate the frequency and intensity of children's internalizing and externalizing symptoms during the first stage of screening; parents also provide a frequency and intensity rating of their children's internalizing and externalizing symptoms. For children identified as at-risk during the first screening stage, teachers and parents separately complete a questionnaire to rate the frequency with which specific symptoms (internalizing and externalizing symptoms and prosocial behavior) occur for children. Children identified as at-risk during the second screening stage are referred for further evaluation.

The BASC-2 BESS and the ASQ-SE are one-stage screeners. Like the PBSS, the BASC-2 BESS involves the use of multiple informants. Parents and teachers separately provide frequency ratings for questions that address internalizing and externalizing problems, as well as children's adaptive skills. A published intervention guide with "tip sheets" for parents on various social-emotional and behavioral concerns is available (Feeney-Kettler, Kratochwill, Kaiser, et al., 2010). The ASQ-SE is also designed for multiple informant participation in screening. It measures seven constructs, including self-regulation, compliance, communication, adaptive functioning, autonomy, affect, and interaction with people. Questions require frequency ratings and vary by age. Given that the ASQ-SE takes 10 to 15 minutes to complete per child, Feeney-Kettler, Kratochwill, Kaiser, et al. (2010) concluded that it may not be appropriate for class-wide universal screening. These same authors recommend spending no more than 10 minutes per student during a universal screening phase to maintain both time and cost efficiency for screening large numbers of students. The ASQ-SE may instead be more appropriate for completion as part of a comprehensive assessment or for targeted assessments of small groups of individual children.

Table 5.1 provides a list of the aforementioned screeners as discussed above, as well as a list of additional screeners, perhaps more appropriate for targeted assessments of smaller numbers of children, given their administration time

TABLE 5.1 Examples of Social-Emotional and Behavioral Screeners

Name of Screener	Informants	Number of Items	Completion Time	Scores
ASEBA[1]	Parent, teacher, or other caregiver	99, additional questions with written answers	10–15 min. per child	Internalizing, externalizing, and total problems; stress problems
ASQ-SE[2]	Parent, teacher, or other caregiver	19–33 (depends on age child)	10–15 min. per child	7 behavioral subscales
BASC-2 BESS[3]	Parent, teacher, or other caregiver		1–2 hours per classroom	Internalizing and externalizing problems, adaptive skills
BASC-2[4]	Parent, teacher, or other caregiver	100 – teacher version; 134 parent version	10–20 minutes per child	Internalizing and externalizing problems; adaptability
ESP[5]	Teacher	Stage 1: nomination rubrics, Stage 2: 41 items	Stages 1 & 2: 1 hour, Stage 3: two 10-min. observations	Internalizing and externalizing disorders; prosocial behavior
PKBS-2[6]	Parent, teacher, or other caregiver	76 items	12 minutes per child	Internalizing and externalizing problems; social skills
PBSS[7]	Parent, teacher, or other caregiver	Phase 1: nomination rubrics, Phase 2: 59 or 60 items	Phase 1: 15–20 min. per classroom, Phase 2: 5–10 min. per identified student	Internalizing and externalizing problems; prosocial behavior

Notes.

[1] *Achenbach System of Empirically Based Assessment* (Achenbach & Rescorla, 2000);
[2] *Ages and Stages Questionnaires: Social Emotional* (ASQ-SE; Squires, Bricker, & Twombly, 2002);
[3] *Behavior and Emotional Screening System* (BASC-2 BESS; Kamphaus & Reynolds, 2007);
[4] *Behavior Assessment System for Children*, 2nd ed. (BASC-2; Reynolds & Kamphaus, 2004);
[5] *Early Screening Project* (ESP; Walker, Severson, & Feil, 1995);
[6] *Preschool and Kindergarten Behavior Scales*, 2nd ed. (PKBS-2; Merrell, 2003);
[7] *Preschool Behavior Screening System* (Feeney-Kettler, Kratochwill, & Kettler, 2012)

requirements. The instruments presented in this table include those that provide a broad assessment of children's social and emotional functioning, rather than on more narrow band or specific areas, such as autism. The target age group is between 3 and 5 years old. It is important to note that this list of instruments to screen for social-emotional and behavioral functioning is not exhaustive. The selected instruments were obtained by reviewing the Mental Measurements Yearbook database, and also the ERIC, PsycINFO, and PsyARTICLES search engines with the keywords *screening, internalizing disorder, externalizing disorder, behavior problems*, and *behavior disorders*.

When Is the Ideal Time to Screen?

The ideal time to screen depends on the preschool or childcare settings' resources. Ideally, screening would occur two times per year, once in the fall and once in the spring, especially since young children's development changes so rapidly. However, if resources do not permit this, screening one time per year is better than not screening at all. It is advisable for children to be in their school or childcare setting a minimum of 30 days before screening. Waiting a period of time for a child to adjust to a new setting, classroom, or teacher, and for the teacher or childcare provider to learn about the child may serve to reduce false positive or false negative identification on screening instruments. Manuals for measures may also specify the length of time that a caregiver is required to know the child prior to completing the screener.

Special Information about Screening the Early Childhood Population

The early childhood population is a special population. All areas of development are very tied together (Powell, Dunlap, & Fox, 2006). For example, physical development, language development, and so on influence social and emotional development. It is important to remember that physical problems or language problems may contribute to symptoms of social-emotional and behavioral problems. For example, one study found that 34.4% of children referred for psychiatric disorders actually had language impairments (Cohen, Davine, Horodezky, Lipsett, & Isaacson, 1993).

Consider the following children who may be identified as at-risk on a social-emotional and behavioral screener. Gabby is often disruptive during center times that require her to color or engage in writing tasks; she has undiagnosed fine motor difficulties and requires occupational therapy support.

Sam rarely follows directions and is irritable; he has an undiagnosed hearing impairment that requires intervention. Brian never seems to pay attention to his teacher; he has an undiagnosed visual impairment and needs glasses. Sariah is very irritable and has frequent meltdowns; she has undiagnosed sleep apnea and is on allergy medication with a possible side effect of irritability and agitation.

In summary, because young children develop so rapidly and because all areas of their development are so intertwined, it is imperative to consider and assess all domains of a child's functioning, including a thorough developmental history, if a screener indicates an elevated risk status for social-emotional and behavioral problems.

Additionally, it is also important to consider environmental variables (e.g., classroom structure, teacher–child relationship, classroom schedule, available activities, peer relationships, etc.) and setting events, such as familial concerns (e.g., a move, divorce, birth of new baby, conflict, parent–child relationship, etc.), as factors that may impact children's social-emotional and behavioral functioning. All of the aforementioned variables must be carefully considered and examined when children are identified as at-risk by a screening instrument.

Integrating Screening into a Multitiered System of Supports

A multitiered system of support is designed to meet the needs of all children, both those with and without social-emotional and behavior problems. At each tier, children are provided with the type of evidence-based support they need to be successful participants in the early childhood setting. Social-emotional and behavior screening can be integrated into a multitiered system of supports. In fact, screening can be used to help determine which students may require additional support, and may also help inform the nature of these supports. Burns and Gibbons (2012) describe how preschool children are screened for early academic skills three times per year. For children below academic target levels, they receive additional instruction, and their progress is monitored more frequently. A similar system could be applied to social-emotional and behavioral screening. Ideally a Tier 1 or core curriculum to promote positive social-emotional and behavioral development is already in place. Children identified as at-risk on a universal social-emotional and behavior screener could receive additional support (Tier 2) targeting the area(s) of social and emotional concern. This support may occur within small groups of children. Progress monitoring of target social and emotional concerns would indicate whether or not children were benefitting from the Tier 2 level supports and whether they required more individualized, evidence-based supports (Tier 3).

Case Example

A case example is used to illustrate the implementation of a social-emotional and behavior screener in a preschool setting. The example highlights some of the preplanning actions previously discussed in this chapter, as well as procedures following the identification of children who may be at-risk for social-emotional and behavioral problems.

Consider the case of Sherman Academy as introduced in Chapter 3. Sherman staff would like to promote the healthy social-emotional and behavioral development of the children at Sherman. The staff wants to implement a school-wide screening program for the 3- to 5-year-old children in the preschool classrooms. There are four preschool classrooms, each containing 15 children. Given the large number of children the staff want to screen for their social-emotional and behavioral functioning, and an assessment of the resources, Sherman determines that a universal screener that takes a minimal amount of time per student would be most appropriate for the school's needs.

Sherman staff reviewed the list of possible social-emotional and behavioral universal screeners. They liked the idea of a multiple stage screener and decided to implement the PBSS, during the next academic year. The director scheduled a workshop for teachers to learn how to administer the PBSS, and a training session for the identified staff members who would score student responses. The school's educational consultant agreed to assist with score interpretation and with providing feedback to parents of children who received scores within the at-risk range. A contract was arranged with a local mental health agency to provide further assessments or preventive interventions for children identified as at-risk who required individualized prevention programming outside of the classroom supports already in place. The educational consultant also agreed to provide professional development to teachers on implementing research-based social-emotional and behavior interventions to support children identified as at-risk. For examples of social-emotional and behavior interventions in the classroom, refer to chapter 6.

Teachers completed PBSS Phase 1 on each child in their classroom by indicating the severity and frequency of children's internalizing and externalizing symptoms. Out of the 60 children screened on PBSS Phase 1, 20 children required further screening using PBSS Phase 2. Teachers completed PBSS Phase 2 by indicating the frequency that children experienced various internalizing and externalizing symptoms, as well as the frequency that they exhibited specific prosocial behaviors. Out of the 20 children screened using PBSS Phase 2, 5 children received scores in the at-risk range, requiring further assessment.

Sherman's director contacted the parents of the children who received scores in the at-risk range during PBSS Phase 2. Meetings were scheduled for parents to meet with the director, the educational consultant, and the classroom teacher to discuss the results of the screener. The children were referred to the local mental health agency for a more comprehensive assessment.

The local mental health agency observed the target children in the classroom, and on the playground. Parent and teacher interviews, including a thorough prenatal and developmental history, and rating scales were implemented to gather information regarding the children's current levels of functioning, strengths, and educational needs. Preventive interventions were recommended based on the comprehensive assessment to better support the target children in the school setting. For example, one target child struggled with high levels of anxiety. Relaxation techniques were practiced in small groups in this child's classroom. Parents were also taught the same relaxation techniques to implement with the child at home. Two other target children manifested difficulty controlling their tempers. The whole class was provided with activities to facilitate the identification of and expression of emotions, as well as direct instruction and practice in problem solving. The two target children received additional individualized instruction and support from their classroom teachers in anger management. Parents of these two target children also received training to practice problem solving and emotional literacy in the home setting.

A progress-monitoring system was utilized to determine when or if additional preventive intervention was necessary. Both the local mental health agency and the educational consultant provided teachers and parents with support in intervention implementation.

Summary

The prevalence of mental health problems among children and adolescents is of concern. Early childhood professionals are in a unique position to help identify young children with or at-risk for social-emotional and behavioral problems through the use of screeners. Implementing a screening program requires familiarity with a screening preplanning process that includes knowledge about available screening instruments and their psychometric characteristics, as well as knowledge about the specific early childhood settings' infrastructure and available resources for screening implementation. The interpretation of screening results requires special attention to linguistic and cultural issues and other areas of young children's development (e.g., physical, sensory, motor, language, etc.) that could be impacting social-emotional and behavioral functioning. Incorporating social-emotional and behavior screening into a multitiered system of evidence-based social-emotional and behavior support could be considered. The ultimate goal is that young children with or at-risk for social-emotional and behavior problems receive the evidence-based preventive interventions necessary to promote positive developmental outcomes both now and in the future.

6

Social-Emotional and Behavioral Interventions and Progress Monitoring

Tiers 1, 2, and 3

Encouraged by the success of their academic MTSS, Sherman Academy wonders if the frameworks they have adopted to support the academic needs of their children could also be useful in better supporting the social-emotional-behavioral needs of their children. In meeting with their educational consultant, Sherman staff report they do not have serious concerns about the social-emotional-behavioral development of the children who attend Sherman Academy, as children typically meet their expectations. However, in sharing that they primarily rely on incidental learning opportunities and address behavioral concerns on a case-by-case basis; they express a desire to learn how to explicitly promote healthy social-emotional-behavioral development of their young children in a more systematic process using data they have collected through their screening practices.

Similar to the multitiered approach to academic interventions presented in Chapter 4, a multitiered approach to addressing young children's social-emotional-behavioral needs can be implemented in early childhood education settings. In fact, some MTSS models of social-emotional-behavioral learning preceded the development of academic multitiered service delivery models for young children. Influenced by positive behavioral interventions and supports (PBIS; PBIS.org, 2012), Building Blocks (Sandall & Schwartz, 2008), and the Pyramid Model (Fox, Carta, Strain, Dunlap, & Hemmeter, 2010; Hemmeter, Ostrosky, & Fox, 2006) are two examples of social-emotional-behavioral MTSS models designed for use with young children. This chapter begins with an overview of the basic tenets of PBIS, Building Blocks, and the Pyramid Model, followed by a discussion of specific components of social-emotional-behavioral MTSS models in early childhood education (i.e., tiered interventions, progress monitoring tools, and treatment integrity). The chapter then concludes with examples of social-emotional-behavioral MTSS models in practice.

School-Wide Positive Behavioral Interventions and Supports (SWPBIS)

SWPBIS is a decision-making framework that promotes optimal academic and behavioral development through systematic teaching and support of prosocial behaviors (PBIS.org, 2012). Similar to the MTSS models first introduced in Chapter 1 and presented throughout this text, the SWPBIS framework is driven by continual data collection (via universal screening and progress monitoring) and a continuum of behavioral supports for all children's needs within a supportive system. The anticipated outcomes of SWPBIS are "teaching and learning environments that are less reactive, aversive, dangerous, and exclusionary, and more engaging, responsive, preventive, and productive; address classroom management and disciplinary issues (e.g., attendance, tardiness, antisocial behavior); improve supports for students whose behaviors require more specialized assistance (e.g., emotional and behavioral disorders, mental health); and most importantly, maximize academic engagement and achievement for all students" (PBIS.org, 2012).

Implementation of SWPBIS involves the availability and provision of supports across multiple tiers. For example, at Tier 1, a SWPBIS team develops between three and five school-wide behavioral expectations (e.g., Be Safe, Be Responsible, Be Respectful) along with a matrix delineating examples of how these expectations look across multiple settings such as classrooms, hallways, buses, cafeterias, restrooms, and playgrounds. The SWPBIS team also develops a plan for how these behaviors will be taught; how behavioral data will be collected; and how appropriate behaviors will be recognized and reinforced. At Tiers 2 and 3, additional supports are provided for children who may require more explicit or frequent teaching or an individualized plan to fully support the development of adaptive behaviors.

Although much of the SWPBIS has been conducted in K-12 settings, studies of SWPBIS implementation in early childhood education settings are also emerging (Benedict, Horner, & Squires, 2007). For example, Benedict et al. (2007) provided consultative support to four preschool classroom teachers and examined both the teachers' use of universal PBIS practices as well as the outcomes in terms of children's problem behaviors. In measuring the percentage of nine universal PBIS practices (a rules poster with three to five positively stated classroom rules, a posted classroom schedule, a classroom matrix of behavioral expectations for each classroom routine, use of a transition signal, use of a warning prior to transitions, use of precorrection, use of an acknowledgment system, a ratio of four positive statements to one negative statement, and use of specific verbal praise), they found an increase in the percentage of universal practices implemented while receiving consultation (52.22%, 50%, 64.44%, and 63.33%) as respectively compared to baseline conditions (39.63%, 14.26%, 35.37%, and 38.52%). However, as the rates of children's problem behaviors were low throughout the study (overall mean of 2.7%), significant decreases in problem behaviors were not observed. These findings suggest these preschool teachers were already implementing universal PBIS practices to some degree prior to this study and that consultation with preschool teachers can enhance the degree to which teachers implement such practices.

The Pyramid Model

The Pyramid Model is an MTSS model based on the principles of PBIS and designed to address the social-emotional-behavioral needs of young children (Fox et al., 2010; Hemmeter et al., 2006). The Pyramid Model was originally conceptualized as a promotion, prevention, and intervention model and is organized across multiple tiers. At the base of the pyramid is an effective workforce consisting of systems and policies that can support evidence-based practices such as continual data collection and the implementation of research-supported instructional strategies and interventions. Once an effective workforce is in place, the following tiers are meant to universally address the needs of all children through nurturing and responsive relationships and high quality supportive environments. Nurturing and responsive relationships between adults, adults and children, and children and their peers are of paramount importance to the healthy development of young children and can be facilitated through encouragement and response to children's play and communication as well as praise of appropriate behaviors. Furthermore, children can also reap the benefits of the relationships adults forge with other children, families, and colleagues.

"Children are less likely to engage in problem behavior when they know what to do, how to do it, and what is expected" (Hemmeter et al., 2006, p. 592): In this vein, it is important to pair nurturing and responsive relationships with high quality supportive environments to promote the social-emotional-behavioral growth of all children. High quality supportive environments explicitly teach children expectations in a safe and engaging environment marked by positive interactions amongst children and between children and adults. Key ingredients of a high quality supportive environment include practices such as engaging learning centers, clear instructions and expectations, and a balanced schedule (Hemmeter et al., 2006).

Although it is to be hoped that the social-emotional-behavioral needs of all children will be met through universal practices, additional supports for children who continue to need help are provided through the next tier of the Pyramid Model, targeted social emotional supports, or explicit instruction of social skills. At this tier, social skills are intentionally taught to children who may have acquired these skills through incidental learning or universal practices. Through direct instruction in small groups or one-on-one, modeling, rehearsal, role-playing, prompting, and providing corrective feedback or praise, children may learn the skills required to successfully interact with others in prosocial ways.

The final tier, intensive intervention, is designed to meet the social-emotional-behavioral needs of children who do not respond as expected to universal practices or secondary supports and continue to need additional supports. At this point, an individualized assessment, usually a functional behavioral assessment, is conducted and used to inform the development of an individualized behavior support plan to directly meet the child's specific behavioral needs. People with whom the child typically interacts (e.g., teachers, parents, family members, administrators) are involved in the assessment and plan development. Once in place, the child's progress is monitored and used to inform continuance, modifications, or termination of the behavior support plan.

Building Blocks

Building Blocks is another MTSS model specifically designed to promote healthy social-emotional-behavioral development of preschool children (Sandall & Schwartz, 2008). This model is especially unique in that it is specifically designed for use with children with disabilities. Through the use of intentional teaching and embedded learning opportunities, the Building Blocks model provides preschool teachers with a framework to help children with disabilities meet their learning goals within a general early childhood education setting.

The base of the Building Blocks program is a high-quality early childhood program that provides a developmentally appropriate learning environment sensitive to each child's needs. In addition to a general high-quality early childhood program, curriculum modifications and adaptations must be provided to include all children in classroom learning activities. Further, through the availability of embedded learning opportunities and explicit, child-focused instructional strategies, children with disabilities will be able to be fully included in the classroom in a mutually meaningful and beneficial manner.

Tier 1 Interventions

An essential component of each of the aforementioned MTSS models is intervention. Though the literature abounds with research-based interventions and programs appropriate for universal, selected, and targeted implementation with young children, a comprehensive review of all programs is beyond the scope of this text. Therefore, descriptions of *program examples* that either show promise or have been adopted by preschools implementing MTSS models and are designed for use with all (Tier 1), some (Tier 2), and a few (Tier 3) young children are provided in the sections below. Additional resources for social-emotional-behavioral interventions in early childhood education settings are provided on the companion website. As well, Hojnoski and Missall (2010) provide an exceptional discussion of assessment and intervention practices used to promote social development in preschool classrooms within a tiered model of service delivery.

Social Skills Improvement System (SSIS) Classwide Intervention Program. The SSIS Classwide Intervention Program is a universal social skills program designed to be administered by classroom teachers to all students in the class (Elliott & Gresham, 2007). The program is composed of 10 units (3 lessons each) with instruction appropriate across different age groups: preschool/kindergarten, early elementary, and upper elementary/middle. Whereas the instruction for preschoolers and kindergartners includes developmentally appropriate materials and activities such as drawing and playing games, instruction for upper elementary and older students involves more discussion-based activities. Furthermore, each lesson is structured around six phases consistent with best practices for instruction: prepare, present, practice, review, assess, and generalize. Parent communication and home–school collaboration are facilitated by letters sent home before the program begins and after it ends, as well as weekly notes throughout the program. The program includes a teacher's guide, student booklets, a resource disc, charts to monitor student progress, certificates of accomplishment, and intervention integrity forms. As well, teachers and schools may wish to adopt the corresponding universal screening tool, the SSIS Performance Screening Guide, to facilitate periodic assessment of young children's social skills. Field-testing indicated that for each lesson, teachers spent approximately 5 to 15 minutes in preparation and 20 to 30 minutes teaching.

Promoting Alternative Thinking Strategies (PATHS). PATHS is a comprehensive social and emotional learning curriculum designed for all children in preschool through sixth grade (Domitrovich, Greenberg, Kusche, & Cortes, 2004). Within a social-cognitive framework, the preschool/kindergarten program promotes the healthy development of self-control, emotional understanding, positive self-esteem, relationships, and interpersonal problem-solving skills. The program is aligned with PBIS and is implemented class wide two to three times per week for approximately 30 minutes. Furthermore, materials that facilitate home–school collaboration and generalization of new skills are available for parents in English and Spanish. Program materials include an instructor's manual, curriculum manual, storybooks, puppets, a feelings chart and feelings card, a poster, stickers, a CD containing materials for parents and a program evaluation tool, and coloring books. The program has been shown to be effective in Head Start classrooms and has been recognized by multiple organizations such as the Substance Abuse and Mental Health Services Administration (SAMHSA); the Collaborative for Academic, Social, and Emotional Learning (CASEL); and the Centers for Disease Control and Prevention (CDC).

Tier 2 Interventions

Social Skills Improvement System (SSIS) Intervention Guide (Elliot & Gresham, 2008). The SSIS *Intervention Guide* is a program designed to promote social competence and the use of prosocial behaviors in children who continue to demonstrate social needs despite receiving Tier 1 interventions such as the aforementioned SSIS Classwide Intervention Program, PATHS, or SWPBIS (Elliott & Gresham, 2008). The program is composed of 20 instructional units within seven domains and is meant to be implemented in small groups or one-on-one outside of the general education classroom by a school psychologist or social worker, for example. Sessions generally occur twice per week for 45 minutes each session, across 15 weeks. Like the *SSIS Classwide Intervention Program*, instruction in the *SSIS Intervention Guide* is organized around the six phases of prepare, present, practice, review, assess, and generalize and is appropriate for use with children of various ages (preschool/kindergarten, early elementary, and upper elementary/middle). Program materials include instruction, student, parent, and evaluation resources. In addition, schools may wish to adopt the corresponding assessment tools, the SSIS Rating Scales (preschool), to facilitate periodic assessment of young children's social skills and problem behaviors.

Tier 3 Interventions

As presented in the discussion of PBIS, the Pyramid Model, and Building Blocks, Tier 3 social-emotional-behavioral interventions are provided for young children who do not show expected progress with Tier 1 and Tier 2 supports. Typically, interventions at this level are embedded in an individualized behavior support plan that is informed by the results of a functional behavioral assessment. The functional behavioral assessment is a focused assessment process that involves the identification of specific behavioral concerns, hypotheses about the function of each behavior (or why it is occurring), and a plan to decrease the identified behaviors and replace them with more adaptive behaviors. For example, if the results of a functional behavioral assessment indicate a child has temper tantrums during free play to receive adult attention, the adults might stop attending to the child when he or he has a temper tantrum, yet attend to the child when he or she plays with other children and does not have a temper tantrum.

Examples of strategies that may be used in a young child's behavior support plan either by structuring an environment that will make desired, prosocial behaviors more likely to occur or by providing consequences that increase the likelihood of prosocial behavior continuing to occur are as follows. Techniques teachers can use to structure an environment that promotes prosocial behaviors include peer-mediated strategies (such as peer initiation, peer tutoring, and peer modeling), cuing/prompting, and precorrection. Conversely, techniques that can provide reinforcing consequences for prosocial behaviors include behavioral contracts, school–home notes, and group-oriented contingency systems (such as the Good Behavior Game). Finally, specific applied behavior analytic techniques (e.g., differential reinforcement) can be used to reduce behaviors of concern (Elliott & Gresham, 2008).

Progress Monitoring of Social-Emotional-Behavioral Outcomes in Young Children

Another essential component of each of the aforementioned MTSS models is assessment. As noted in Chapter 5, assessing the social-emotional-behavioral development of young children can be tricky. In particular, given the developmental levels of young children, many behaviors that might be considered problematic for older children at school are completely adaptive for young children at school. As such, just as social-emotional-behavioral interventions used in MTSS models at the elementary school level cannot be automatically applied to early childhood education settings, nor can universal screening or progress monitoring practices. Instead, progress monitoring practices and tools must be carefully selected to meet the needs of the young children being assessed. This section will provide an overview of progress monitoring practices and select progress monitoring tools.

In elementary and secondary schools, one of the primary methods of monitoring students' behavioral outcomes within a multitiered system of supports is by the frequency and types of office discipline referrals (ODRs) and behavior incident reports (BIRs) over time. Another method of monitoring progress on a daily basis is through the use of individual behavior charts/contracts and point sheets developed specifically for individual students' behavioral needs and aligned with Tier 2 and Tier 3 supports (students who are only receiving universal Tier 1 supports are usually assessed through universal screening, rather than progress monitoring).

Although ODRs/BIRs can also be used as a means to monitor student progress in preschools, they may not prove as useful given the wide range of behaviors that are considered acceptable in early childhood education settings. For example, a high school student might accumulate several ODRs in a relatively short period of time for behaviors he or she is expected to know not to engage in, such as being tardy, being disrespectful to teachers, or not being prepared in class. However, preschool children are unlikely to regularly accumulate ODRs because the expectation is that they are learning how to behave appropriately in positive environments not ridden with punitive consequences. As such, ODRs in preschool are typically acquired for quite serious, low-incidence offenses and may be better used as one method of progress monitoring, rather than the primary method. In contrast, daily point systems and behavior charts could be an ideal method of consistently monitoring the social-emotional-behavioral progress of young children receiving Tier 1, 2, and 3 supports, as these systems can be tailored for class-wide or individual use.

Additional Tools to Monitor the Progress of Social-Emotional-Behavioral Development in Preschool Children

In addition to ODRs/BIRs and class-wide or individual point systems and behavior charts, the social-emotional-behavioral progress of young children receiving Tier 2 and Tier 3 supports could be periodically monitored with commercially available tools. Because some of these tools were not specifically designed to provide formative assessment data, they may require longer administration times, may not be sensitive to small changes in short periods of time, and should only be administered as frequently as indicated in respective manuals to supplement the progress monitoring data that are collected more frequently. Below, two norm-referenced tools are presented, followed by additional observational tools.

Social Skills Improvement System Rating Scales (SSIS-RS). The SSIS-RS, one component of the comprehensive Social Skills Improvement System, provides a method for teachers and parents to monitor children's social-emotional-behavioral progress (Gresham & Elliott, 2008). The SSIS-RS are standardized, norm-referenced instruments designed for use with children 3 to 18 years of age. Meant for use as a Tier 2 assessment tool, the preschool rating scales facilitate measurement of social skills and problem behaviors and can be completed by teachers and parents of young children. The system includes rating scales for preschool, elementary, and secondary-aged children, are available in English and Spanish, and have been shown to be psychometrically sound instruments (Gresham & Elliott, 2008). The Pearson Assessments website provides additional information and resources for the SSIS-RS and the SSIS Performance Screening Guides, tools that can be used in conjunction with the SSIS-RS as universal screeners (see www.pearsonas-sessments.com).

BASC-2 Progress Monitor. The *BASC-2 Progress Monitor* instruments are another standardized, norm-referenced method for monitoring the social-emotional-behavioral functioning of preschoolers (Reynolds & Kamphaus, 2009). The preschool forms include 15 to 20 items designed to measure the behavioral and emotional functioning of young children (as young as 2 years of age) within a few minutes and may be used in conjunction with the comprehensive BASC-2 rating scales. Based on the areas of concern, the Externalizing and ADHD Problems, Internalizing Problems, Social Withdrawal, and Adaptive Skills forms may be completed by teachers and parents for preschool-aged children. Although the frequency of administration is primarily determined by the intervention that is being implemented, the forms can be administered as often as every 2 to 4 weeks to effectively monitor children's progress. The instruments are available in English and Spanish and have been shown to be psychometrically sound (Reynolds & Kamphaus, 2009). The Pearson Assessments website provides additional information and resources for the *BASC-2 Progress Monitor* (see www.pearsonassessments.com).

Teaching Strategies GOLD Assessment System. The *Teaching Strategies GOLD Assessment System* is a comprehensive observational system that is aligned with the Common Core State Standards, state early learning guidelines, and the Head Start Child Development and Early Learning Framework (Teaching Strategies, 2010a). The system facilitates measurement of 10 areas of development and learning, including social-emotional, physical, language, cognitive, literacy, mathematics, science and technology, social studies, the arts, and English language acquisition. With regard to social-emotional development, this system offers a means to measure the ability to regulate emotions and behaviors (dimensions: manages feelings, follows limits and expectations, takes care of own needs appropriately), establish and sustain positive relationships (dimensions: forms relationships with adults, responds to emotional cues, interacts with peers, makes friends), and participate cooperatively and constructively in group situations (dimensions: balances needs and rights of self and others, solves social problems). Through online supports, the assessment system guides teachers through ongoing data collection via observations, data analysis, data interpretation, and data management. The system is also appropriate for use with dual-language learners and children with disabilities. The Teaching Strategies website provides additional information and resources for the *Teaching Strategies GOLD Assessment System* (see www. teachingstrategies.com).

mCLASS+. The mCLASS+ system, introduced and described in chapter 3, is another option for gathering observational progress monitoring data on young children's social-emotional-behavioral development, as the observables facilitate specific measurement of social development. Through the use of a mobile device such as a PDA, teachers use a checklist to record observed social behaviors such as "Engages in activities positively with peers" and "Engages in conversation with peers" on a scale of 1 (seldom) to 5 (often). The Social Assessment observables are conducted three times per year (approximately one month following universal screening), thereby allowing teachers to keep track of children's social interactions with peers over time. The Children's Learning Institute and Wireless Generation websites provide additional information and resources for mCLASS+ (see www.childrenslearninginstitute.org; www.wirelessgeneration.com).

Early Learning Observation and Rating Scale (ELORS). The ELORS, introduced and described in Chapter 3, is another observation system that can be used to monitor the social-emotional-behavioral growth of young children (Gillis, West, & Coleman, 2010a, 2010b). Of particular relevance to children's social-emotional-behavioral development are the self-management and the social and emotional domains. Within the self-management domain, the following behaviors may be observed and recorded: adjusting to changes in routine, following the daily classroom or home schedule, transitioning from one activity to another, consistency of behavior or mood, understanding the consequences of behaviors, using planning prior to activities, persisting on difficult tasks, paying attention during group activities, using words to solve problems with peers, and concentrating for brief periods of time. In addition, the social and emotional domain facilitates measurement of the extent to which children make friends, play cooperatively with other children, participate in social activities, use turn-taking in play, label emotions of others, express anger appropriately, express frustration appropriately, function independently of adult attention, maintain friendships, and show a range of emotions (Gillis et al., 2010a, 2010b). The Get Ready to Read website provides additional information and resources for the ELORS (see www. getreadytoread.org).

While an early childhood education setting such as Sherman Academy is developing an assessment plan (including universal screening and progress monitoring), the site must also develop decision rules or guidelines for movement between the tiers. Although some sources do offer guidance for creating such decision rules (e.g., students who have received a certain number of ODRs within a certain period of time will receive Tier 2 supports), such decisions can appear arbitrary if the context of the site and each individual's growth are not considered. As such, sites may wish to be aware of such guidelines (often provided with the selected progress monitoring tools) for use in conjunction with variables such as school/class expectations and individual performance. It may also behoove sites to conceptualize movement across tiers as a fluid process, acknowledging that supports across the tiers are essentially available for all children at any time.

Tiered Social-Emotional-Behavioral Interventions in Practice

Several MTSS models of academic learning and instructional practices of were presented in Chapter 4. As with models of academic learning, tiered models of social-emotional-behavioral learning are also in various stages of implementation. Below, social-emotional-behavioral interventions and progress monitoring practices used in three Illinois school districts are presented.

Rockford Public Schools Early Childhood Program. The Rockford Early Childhood Program serves children 3 to 5 years of age across nine elementary schools, Roosevelt Community Education Center, Dennis Early Education Center, Fairview Early Childhood Center, two local childcare centers, and one Head Start center in Rockford, Illinois (National Center for Learning Disabilities [NCLD], 2009). Whereas some sites are currently implementing MTSS models to address the academic or behavioral needs of their young children, the Rockford program is unique in that it promotes healthy development in both the academic and social-emotional-behavioral domains within a tiered framework. Following an initial screening with the *Early Screening Inventory—Revised* and the *Ages and Stages Questionnaire—Social-Emotional*, the program conducts universal screening four times a year with Work Sampling Illinois and behavioral data. With regard to prevention and intervention, the program implements three curricula: High/Scope Preschool Curriculum, Second Step Violence Prevention, and Woven Word dialogic reading and social-emotional development program. As the program evolves,

Tier 2 supports will include supplemental instruction, and Tier 3 supports will include intensive instruction and intervention.

Glenview Public School District #34. The Glenview Early Childhood Program is located in Glenview, Illinois (Brown & Tom, 2012). Like the Rockford program, the Glenview program addresses both the academic and social-emotional-behavioral needs of young children. The program serves approximately 170 children in a variety of classrooms (blended, self-contained, prekindergarten, and bilingual/Spanish). Driven by state mandates requiring each school district to create an RTI plan and also address the state's social-emotional-learning standards, the Glenview Early Childhood Program developed a MTSS model to meet the social-emotional-behavioral learning needs of their young children through assessment, intervention, and teaming. With regard to assessment of social-emotional-behavioral development, children's strengths and needs are regularly assessed and monitored in accordance with the social development objectives of the Creative Curriculum, the program's core curriculum. In addition to the Creative Curriculum, social/behavioral interventions in Tier 1 include The Incredible Years and parent-teacher-child interaction therapy, as well as general classroom behavior management strategies and practices such as picture icons, social stories, classroom schedule, cues, and prompts. Tier 2 interventions include targeted behavior management, Second Step, specific incentives, video modeling, and buddy box. Finally, Tier 3 interventions include direct instruction for task completion, errorless learning for teaching new skills, and discrete trial format for specific behaviors and play. In support of this model, teaming occurs biweekly through Professional Learning Communities.

Prairie Children Preschool. As introduced in Chapter 4, Prairie Children Preschool is a community preschool of the Indian Prairie School District #204 in Aurora, Illinois (Young, Snow, Frech, & Shields, 2011). In blending the Creative Curriculum for Preschool, PBIS, and PATHS, the Prairie Children Preschool has a comprehensive set of Tier 1 practices. Components of PBIS are infused with the Creative Curriculum at Prairie Children Preschool through the consistent implementation of "expectations" across settings and the use of strategies such as Cool Tools, visual supports, visual schedules combined with verbal prealert statements, transition signals, precorrection, reinforcement, Positive Patches, and Game Days. The program later added PATHS to foster the development of prosocial skills, initially led by school psychologists and school social workers as a Tier 2 intervention with select children, and later as a Tier 1 practice conducted by classroom teachers with all children. Behavioral progress is monitored at least monthly via behavioral data. In addition, prosocial behaviors are monitored at least twice a year with a PATHS-specific tool. Data are also collected via the Creative Curriculum.

Summary

Creating a school/classroom environment that fosters optimal social-emotional-behavioral growth for all young children is absolutely essential in early childhood education settings, as early social-emotional-behavioral development lays the foundation for each child's development into a socially healthy child, adolescent, and adult. MTSS models can offer a systematic way for educators to provide a continuum of supports matched to each child's needs that are data-driven through assessment practices such as universal screening and progress monitoring. This chapter provided a basic introduction to early childhood models of social-emotional-behavioral MTSS, as well as examples of interventions and progress monitoring tools at each tier. In practice, the specific context and culture of the site and the needs of its students will drive the development of the model. Furthermore, implementing such a model will require extensive planning and teaming, as well as ongoing evaluations of implementation integrity.

7

Developmental Disability Identification and Considerations for Inclusion

Early childhood is an exciting period of rapid, variable development in which most children will demonstrate skills consistent with broad age-based expectations. The vast majority of children in early childhood education programs will likely meet the general expectations of the universal curriculum and standards or local norms on which the program is based. For the minority of children who exhibit delayed or atypical developmental trajectories, early childhood professionals can play a critical role in screening for possible developmental delays, identifying the nature of apparent delays or qualitative differences, and, when appropriate, identifying or diagnosing developmental disabilities.

This chapter provides an overview of typical developmental milestones during early childhood that can serve as a general framework for considering age-based developmental expectations. It also includes steps that can be taken when a child does not seem to be meeting developmental milestones or is showing signs of atypical development. Practical points are offered for consideration when assessing and identifying developmental delays, including cultural and linguistic considerations. Case examples are provided at the conclusion of the chapter. This chapter is not intended to provide the advanced training required to identify or diagnose specific developmental disabilities. Rather, it is intended as an overview of issues related to the identification of developmental delays and disabilities in the context of early childhood education programs and considerations for including young children with developmental differences in general education programs. Resources for accessing information to further explore these issues are included in the *Early Childhood Education* companion website.

Early Childhood Developmental Milestones

As is apparent to early childhood education professionals, there is a wide range of typical development during this period. Nonetheless, it can be helpful for those working with young children to be familiar with developmental milestones on which to base their general expectations for typical development. Developmental milestones represent skills that most children will exhibit by a specified age. Not reaching a developmental milestone by a certain age does not necessarily mean that a child has a disability or disorder. Ample opportunity to practice a skill is necessary for young children to meet most developmental milestones.

Developmental milestones for children ages 2 to 5 can be categorized into broad domains such as communication, cognitive, motor, self-care, and social skills. Although there is considerable overlap among these categories (e.g., communication and social skills, cognitive and self-care skills), it can be helpful to consider a child's developmental profile across multiple domains of functioning. Most children will meet age-based milestones across each of these areas, while some children may be delayed in meeting milestones in one or more of the broad domains. A reference chart of typical developmental milestones can be found on the *Early Childhood Education* companion website.

Communication Milestones

Communication milestones include both receptive (understanding of) and expressive (use of) language skills. In the area of receptive language, many children are able to follow two-step instructions by 2 to 3 years of age, answer simple *wh*-questions by 3 to 4 years of age, and recall part of a story by age 4 to 5 years. In the area of expressive language, many children are able to name most objects by 2 to 3 years of age, frequently use sentences with four or more words by 3 to 4 years of age, and use the same grammar as the rest of his or her family by age 4 to 5. Below are examples of skills that most children are able to do in each of the specified age ranges (American Academy of Pediatrics [AAP], 2004; American Speech-Language-Hearing Association, n.d.):

Ages 2 to 3

- Understand differences in meaning of simple words (e.g., "stop" and "go")
- Follow two-step requests
- Point to a familiar object, or picture of an object, when it is named
- Know first and last name
- Have a word to label most objects
- Use two- to three-word sentences
- Use speech that is understood by familiar people most of the time
- Ask for objects, or direct attention to objects, by naming them

Ages 3 to 4

- Understand concepts of "same" and "different"
- Follow three-step requests
- Answer simple *wh*-questions
- Talk about play or school activities
- Use speech that is understood by unfamiliar people
- Use many sentences with four or more words
- Talk easily without repeating syllables or words
- Have mastered some basic rules of grammar
- Tell stories

Ages 4 to 5

- Understand most of what is said at home and at school
- Pay attention to short stories and answer simple questions about the story
- Use sentences with a lot of detail
- Tell stories that stay on topic
- Communicate easily with other children and adults
- Say most sounds correctly
- Say rhyming words
- Name some letters and numbers
- Use the same grammar as the rest of the family
- Use future tense
- Say name and address

Cognitive Milestones

Cognitive milestones during early childhood include developing skills such as categorizing items by shape and color, counting, and understanding the functions of common objects. By ages 2 to 3, many children are able to match an object to a picture of the object and understand the concepts of "same" and "different" by ages 3 to 4. Many 4- to 5-year old children can count at least 10 objects. The following is a summary of general cognitive milestones for ages 2 through 5 (AAP, 2004):

Ages 2 to 3
- Match an object to a picture of the object
- Sort objects by shape and color
- Complete 3- to 4-piece puzzles
- Understand concept of "two" (e.g., two blocks)

Ages 3 to 4
- Correctly name some colors
- Understand the concept of counting and may know a few numbers
- Begin to have a clearer sense of time

Ages 4 to 5
- Count at least 10 objects
- Correctly name at least four colors
- Better understand the concept of time
- Know about things used every day in the home (e.g., money, food, appliances)

Motor and Self-Care Milestones

Motor milestones involve skills requiring the use of larger muscle groups (i.e., gross motor skills) and smaller muscle groups (i.e., fine motor skills). Some of these skills allow for young children to becoming increasingly involved in self-care activities, such as eating and toileting independently. By ages 2 to 3, many children demonstrate gross motor skills such as kicking a ball or jumping and fine motor skills such as stacking small blocks. When children reach ages 3 to 4, many are able to engage in gross motor activities such as standing on one foot and fine motor activities such as using scissors and drawing circles and squares. By ages 4 to 5, many children can dress and undress without assistance and print some letters in the alphabet. Below are representative skills that most children in these specific age ranges have developed (AAP, 2004; Parlakian & Lerner, 2008; Patrick, Spear, Holt, & Sofka, 2001):

Ages 2 to 3
- Climb well
- Walk up and down stairs while alternating feet
- Walk backward
- Kick a ball
- Run easily
- Pedal a tricycle
- Bend over easily without falling
- Gallop and jump
- Make vertical, horizontal, and circular strokes with a crayon
- Turn book pages one-at-a-time
- Build a six-block tower
- Hold a crayon or pencil in a writing position
- Screw and unscrew jar lids
- Turn rotating handles

Ages 3 to 4
- Hop and stand on one foot for up to 5 seconds
- Walk up and down stairs without support
- Kick a ball forward
- Throw a ball overhand
- Catch a bounced ball most of the time
- Move forward and backward with agility
- Copy square shapes
- Draw a person with two to four body parts
- Use scissors
- Draw circles and squares
- Begin to copy some capital letters
- Dress and undress (may need some assistance)
- Use the toilet (may need some assistance)

Ages 4 to 5
- Stand on one foot for at least 10 seconds
- Do a somersault
- Swing
- May be able to skip
- Copy triangles and other simple geometric forms
- Draw a person with a body

- Print some letters
- Use a fork and spoon well
- Dress and undress without assistance
- Usually care for own toileting needs independently

Social Milestones

Social milestones during early childhood reflect skills developed in areas such as interpersonal relationships and play. Many children can take turns in games by ages 2 to 3 and cooperate with other children by ages 3 to 4. When children reach ages 4 to 5, many want to please their friends and will show concern for others. Below are examples of social skills that most children in each of the specified age ranges have acquired (AAP, 2004):

Ages 2 to 3
- Imitate adults and other children
- Show affection for familiar playmates
- Can take turns in games
- Understand concepts of "mine" and "his or hers"
- Make-believe play with dolls, animals, or figurines

Ages 3 to 4
- Interested in new experiences
- Cooperate with other children
- Increasingly inventive in fantasy play
- Negotiate solutions to conflicts

Ages 4 to 5
- Want to please and be like their friends
- Are more likely to agree to rules
- Are aware of their gender
- Show concern for others
- Start to distinguish fantasy from reality

In addition to the absence of particular skills by a specific age, the presence of certain behaviors may be an indication of atypical development that warrants further attention. For example, it can be useful for early childhood professionals to be familiar with general characteristics of play that may be associated with cognitive delays. Compared to same-age peers, children with cognitive delays may exhibit play that is characterized by (Vig & Sanders, 2007, p. 435):

1. Interest in physical, rather than representational, properties of toys
2. More time spent in nonspecific manipulation (holding, fingering, sliding, throwing)
3. Less sustained involvement with toys
4. Less varied play schemas
5. More repetition
6. Fewer toys combined
7. Fewer sequential combinations of toys
8. Less elaboration of play themes

Steps to Take When a Child Is Showing Signs of Developmental Delay or Atypical Development

While most children will meet general developmental milestones by the expected ages, some children will not. Early childhood education professionals have an important role in identifying developmental delays and connecting families with early intervention services outside the classroom, as well as facilitating a child's individual development within the classroom. When questions arise regarding a child's development, early childhood educators can gather information regarding the child's current behavior or skills in comparison to expected developmental milestones. This can be done through the use of universal screening, direct observation, and progress-monitoring techniques discussed in Chapters 3, 4, 5, and 6. It is recommended that the following steps be implemented in the context of a multitiered system of supports; they are not intended to replace the addition of increasingly intensive classroom interventions, as needed.

Discuss the Developmental Concerns with the Child's Parents or Guardians. If an early childhood education professional is concerned about a child's development, discussing these concerns and the basis for them, with the child's parents or guardians is an important first step. The results of a study on communicating with parents about developmental delays in primary care medical settings suggests that it may be beneficial to prepare parents for accepting information related to suspected delays by giving them information regarding expected developmental milestones, suggestions for promoting skill development, and a specific time frame for follow-up evaluation

(Sices, Egbert, & Mercer, 2009). Some of the themes and resulting recommendations from this study could be applicable to similar situations in an early childhood educational setting: (a) considering parents' level of awareness of developmental concerns when choosing to use a nonalarmist style or a more direct approach for discussing possible or suspected delays; (b) preparing parents by providing them with information regarding emerging skills to look for and to discuss at a follow-up appointment, if appropriate; (c) communicating to parents the importance of any concerns they may have; (d) anticipating that parents may feel blamed for their child's developmental delay and address this concern directly; and (e) providing appropriate referral information, involving parents as members of the evaluation team, and staying involved after a referral has been made (Sices et al., 2009).

It is also critical to consider the influence of culture on parents' beliefs regarding early childhood development and parents' roles, as well as the role of early childhood education professionals, in facilitating skill development in young children. Cultural variations in expectations for young children's development and parenting practices have been well documented (Maschinot, 2008; National Research Council and Institute for Medicine, 2000). Certain developmental milestones may not align with a particular family's expectations for their child. For example, some families may not expect a 3-year-old child to use the toilet. As a result, the child may not have had the opportunity to practice the skills that many of his or her peers had developed by the same age. Exploring families' individual and cultural beliefs regarding early childhood developmental milestones is an essential piece of examining a child's possible developmental delay.

Encourage Parents to Talk to Their Child's Health Care Provider. As part of the process of identifying possible developmental delays or disabilities, parents should be encouraged to seek consultation from their child's health care provider. Some delays and disabilities may have identifiable medical or genetic causes (e.g., Fragile X syndrome), require physical examination for diagnosis (e.g., cerebral palsy), or have associated medical problems that require attention. In addition, access to some types of evaluation and treatment services in the community may require the referral of a primary health care provider.

Refer for Early Intervention: Evaluation for Children under 3 years of Age. For children under the age of 3, early childhood education professionals should assist with connecting families to Early Intervention services, which are available to eligible children from birth to age 3 under Part C of the Individuals with Disabilities Education Improvement Act (IDEA). Research has shown that an estimated 13% of young children have developmental delays that would make them eligible for such services; however, it is estimated that only 10% of eligible children receive early intervention services at 24 months of age (Rosenberg, Zhang, & Robinson, 2008). African American children, in particular, are significantly less likely to receive these services as compared to children from other racial/ethnic groups (Rosenberg et al., 2008). Early childhood education professionals can help reduce such disparities by assisting parents with accessing intervention services for which their child is eligible. Eligibility criteria vary by state, so it is important for early childhood education personnel to be familiar with their state's general criteria and the lead agency in their state that is designated to implement eligibility evaluations and programming for Early Intervention services.

Refer for Early Childhood Special Education: Evaluation for Children 3 to 5 Years of Age. For children ages 3 through 5, educators in private early childhood programs should help connect families to their local public school district for an evaluation to determine eligibility for early childhood special education services under Part B of IDEA. Education personnel in public early childhood and prekindergarten programs can follow their school district's procedures for referring a child for an evaluation. Again, such a referral can be made in the context of a multitiered system of supports and continued monitoring of a child's response to interventions in the general classroom.

Practical Tips and Considerations for Assessment and Evaluation of Developmental Delays

Clarify the Purpose of the Developmental Assessment. Before assessing for developmental delays, it is necessary to clarify the purpose of the assessment. For example, is the purpose to conduct a universal developmental screening for all children in an early childhood program, to assess fine motor skills in a child who seems to be struggling in this area, or to determine whether a child has a disability and is in need of early childhood special education services under the educational classification of autism? Clarifying the purpose of the assessment allows for the assessor or assessment team to focus on relevant considerations for the intended goals. An example of a relevant consideration in the context of an evaluation for early childhood special education eligibility is the overlap and distinction between the *Diagnostic and Statistical Manual of Mental Disorders* (DSM-IV; American Psychiatric Association, 2000) or other diagnostic criteria used in clinical and medical settings and educational disability criteria under IDEA. A child with a clinical or medical diagnosis of an autism spectrum disorder, for example, may not necessarily be found to be eligible for early childhood special education services under the disability classification of autism due to the differences in criteria between diagnostic/classification systems. General considerations for conducting universal screenings in early childhood education programs can be found in Chapters 3 and 5.

Gather Information from Multiple Sources Using Multiple Assessment Methods. The importance of collecting information from multiple sources and methods becomes increasingly important as one moves along the continuum from universal screening to targeted assessment to diagnostic or special education eligibility evaluation. At the diagnostic or disability determination end of this continuum, gathering assessment information across settings is also imperative. Sources of information may include parents, the child, teachers, or the child's health care provider. Assessment methods may include direct observation, interviews, standardized performance-based instruments, or informant rating scales. Relevant settings may include the early childhood classroom, home, playground, or community. Collectively, information from multiple sources, methods, and settings can best capture a picture of the whole child and his or her functioning in a particular developmental domain.

Consider Relevant Cultural and Linguistic Issues. In the context of an assessment or evaluation of developmental delays, relevant cultural factors that should be taken into consideration include the family's: (a) perspective on how the child is functioning based on their developmental expectations;(b) views on disability; (c) views on the roles of families and professionals in the evaluation process; (d) goals for early intervention; and (e) communication styles (Brassard & Boehm, 2007; Zhang & Bennett, 2003). Linguistic considerations in the context of early childhood assessment that are relevant to evaluations of developmental delay include establishing a child's linguistic background, assessing a child's language proficiency, and hiring and training staff members for linguistic and cultural diversity (Brassard & Boehm, 2007). In the context of special education evaluations for English language learners, Ortiz and Yates (2002) offer the following general guidelines:

1. Assess in both languages.
2. Use equivalent instruments and procedures in the native language and in English.
3. When testing only in English, establish the student's level of English proficiency.
4. Use valid and reliable instruments.
5. Determine appropriate adaptations of instruments and procedures.

Gather Information that Can Inform Intervention, Including a Child's Strengths. Evaluations should be focused on obtaining information that will be useful for designing and implementing interventions, rather than merely providing a diagnostic label. In addition to understanding the areas in which a child may need further development, it is important to assess a child's strengths and environmental and family risk and protective factors (Brassard & Boehm, 2007). Taken together, evaluation of these areas can help provide a developmental picture of the whole child as to what types of intervention programming would be most helpful in fostering his or her development.

Practical Considerations for Inclusion of Children with Developmental Disabilities

The Division for Early Childhood (DEC) of the Council for Exceptional Children and the National Association for the Education of Young Children (NAEYC) have released a joint position statement that offers the following definition of early childhood inclusion:

> Early childhood inclusion embodies the values, policies, and practices that support the right of every infant and young child and his or her family, regardless of ability, to participate in a broad range of activities and contexts as full members of families, communities, and society. The desired results of inclusive experiences for children with and without disabilities and their families include a sense of belonging and membership, positive social relationships and friendships, and development and learning to reach their full potential. The defining features of inclusion that can be used to identify high quality early childhood programs and services are access, participation, and supports. (DEC & NAEYC, 2009, p. 2)

This position statement argues that high quality early childhood inclusion programs are characterized by the provision of access to a variety of activities, educational opportunities, and environments. Principles of universal design can be used to remove barriers to access to the general curriculum for children with disabilities. Individualized accommodations and the use of adaptive technology can facilitate participation for all students in the general curriculum and classroom. These inclusion strategies can be implemented in the context of multitiered system of supports with necessary systems-level supports and ongoing professional development for staff. The DEC and NAEYC (2009, pp. 3–4) recommend that this position statement, which can serve as a framework for conceptualizing inclusive early childhood education programs, be used to achieve the following general goals:

1. Create high expectations for every child to reach his or her full potential.
2. Develop a program philosophy on inclusion.
3. Establish a system of services and supports.
4. Revise program and professional standards.
5. Achieve an integrated professional development system.
6. Influence federal and state accountability systems.

Promoting a Culture of Inclusion. Promoting a culture of inclusion is the foundation of successful inclusive early childhood education programming. Staff, students, parents, and the larger community all contribute to the culture of an early childhood program and can all be considered stakeholders in the success of efforts to include children with developmental disabilities. In addition to facilitating the meaningful participation of children with disabilities in a general education curriculum and environment, inclusion can be thought of as a way to include *all* students from diverse cultural, economic, and linguistic backgrounds. Special considerations arise when considering strategies for promoting the inclusion of students with disabilities who are also English language learners or represent diverse racial, ethnic, or cultural backgrounds. Cloud (2002) highlights approaches for creating culturally responsive teaching and learning environments in the context of educating English language learners with disabilities:

• Select curricular themes and instructional materials that acknowledge the life experiences and background knowledge of the students.
• Recognize that students' expectations about classroom interactions vary greatly both among and within cultures.

- Choose teaching approaches that are compatible with students' preferences and prior learning experiences.
- Use resources such as times, space, and people in ways that are sensitive to students.
- Recognize that parent outreach efforts need to be sensitive to students' cultural backgrounds.

Professional Development and Training for Staff. Preservice training and ongoing professional development for early childhood educators is critical for the success of inclusive programming. A study by Bruns and Mogharreban (2007) found that most Head Start and prekindergarten teachers in their sample believe that children with disabilities should receive services in early childhood settings alongside their same-age peers and identified three chief topics for professional development related to inclusion: behavioral issues, communication strategies, and handling and positioning of students. In their review of effective educational programming for children with autism spectrum disorders, the National Research Council (2001) highlighted the need for professional development related to the course of ASD, the range of possible outcomes, and best practice educational methods. To effectively engage in evidence-based practices related to early childhood education for children with developmental disabilities, Carta and Kong (2007, p. 193) note that early childhood education professionals need ongoing training and technical assistance that:

1. focuses on the best available information, including easy-to-access and highly reliable summaries of effective intervention procedures and programs;
2. develops multiple methods for distributing this information in forms well suited to particular audiences;
3. and pairs information distribution with focused, effective professional development interventions in ways that make it easier, and much more likely, that procedures will be adopted in various settings.

The *Early Childhood Education* companion website includes a list of resources that can be used to obtain or develop training materials related to inclusion of children with developmental disabilities.

Integrating Inclusion into a Multitiered System of Supports. Multitiered systems of supports are intended to meet the needs of *all* students, so inclusion of children with developmental disabilities is consistent with this service delivery framework. At each tier, students are provided the level of support they need to be successful learners. Carta and Kong (2007) describe three broad types of instructional supports that can be used to individualize instruction based on a child's level of need. First, the environment can be shaped in ways that offer opportunities for a child to practice certain skills. For example, the types of materials available, the amount of space, the sequence of activities, or the number of adults and peers present can be directly manipulated to facilitate skill development and positive behavior. A second type of instructional support is the use of specialized procedures, such as responsive-interaction strategies, naturalistic teaching strategies, and reinforcement-based procedures (Carta & Kong, 2007). Multiple types of intervention procedures and instructional supports can be integrated into multitiered early childhood instructional models to facilitate the growth of all children, including those with developmental disabilities.

Case Examples

Anthony. Anthony is 2 years old and attends a childcare program at a local community center three days per week. His child care teachers have noticed that he does not seem to be meeting general developmental milestones and is showing some atypical behaviors. In particular, they are concerned that he does not yet use two-word sentences or follow most verbal instructions. Anthony's teachers have also noticed that he does not interact much with the other children or make eye contact when someone is speaking to him, and often lines up toys and other materials in a row rather than using them as they are intended.

The program director called Anthony's parents to discuss his development. The director, Anthony's lead teacher, and his parents met the following week. Anthony's teacher shared her observations of how Anthony seemed to be having difficulty with his communication skills and did not seem to be interested in the other children in his classroom. Anthony's parents mentioned that they had noticed similar behaviors but wondered if he was just behaving typically for a boy, as their older child is a girl. The director recommended that Anthony's parents discuss these concerns with his pediatrician at his next visit. The director also explained that Anthony could receive a developmental evaluation from the state's Early Intervention program and, if found to be eligible, could receive special services at home to help promote his development.

Anthony's parents had not heard of this service and were interested in pursuing an evaluation. Anthony's teacher and the program director also discussed with Anthony's parents strategies they could use at the childcare center to help him make gains in his communication and social skills. They decided, in collaboration with Anthony's parents, to provide some additional supports in the classroom, such as adult support to facilitate peer interactions and modeling developmentally appropriate play with toys that were of interest to him. The director asked Anthony's parents to return for a follow-up meeting after they had talked with Anthony's pediatrician about his development and completed the evaluation for Early Intervention services.

Anthony's parents returned for a follow-up meeting with the childcare program director and Anthony's teacher 2 months later. They reported that Anthony's pediatrician said that Anthony is showing some signs of a possible autism spectrum disorder and made a referral for him to have a diagnostic evaluation at a developmental disabilities clinic. Anthony's parents also stated that Anthony was evaluated by the state's Early Intervention program and will soon begin receiving speech-language therapy at home. Anthony's parents and the childcare program staff agreed that it would be best to collaborate with his Early Intervention service coordinator to make a plan for supporting his development at daycare.

Mia. Mia is 4 years old and attends a 4-year-old kindergarten (4K) program through her local school district. This is her first experience with early childhood education outside of the home. Mia's teacher observed that Mia did not seem to be meeting the developmental milestones that the other students in the class had achieved. Mia was having difficulty following two-step instructions, did not seem to understand the concept of counting, and could not identify any colors, letters, or numbers by name. She was also having difficulty copying simple shapes. Mia's teacher noticed that her expressive language appeared to be much less developed compared to her peers. The results of a universal screening for preacademic skills revealed that Mia was not performing at the level of most of her classmates.

Mia's teacher added some additional supports for Mia, such as providing the whole class with increased opportunities to work on fine motor skills, such as drawing shapes, during center-based activities. During their daily literacy period, her teacher paired Mia with a classmate who would often name colors and objects that she saw in books, as well as count items in books.

Mia's teacher thought that Mia could benefit from more intensive supports in the classroom, so she initiated an evaluation to determine whether Mia had a disability and was in need of special education services. The multidisciplinary evaluation team conducted classroom and playground observations; standardized, norm-referenced assessments; a parent interview; and utilized parent- and teacher-completed rating scales to gather information regarding Mia's current level of development across several domains, strengths, and her educational needs. It was determined that Mia was eligible to receive special education services under the early childhood classification of Developmental Delay. An Individualized Education Program (IEP) was developed for Mia and she began to receive more intensive supports in the classroom, including individualized instruction in the general education classroom from the school's speech-language therapist and occupational therapist, as well as an early childhood special education teacher. Mia continued to participate in the general education curriculum and the progress-monitoring system that her school utilized to determine when additional instructional support was warranted.

Summary

Early childhood education professionals are in a unique position to help identify children with developmental delays or disabilities. Doing so requires familiarity with general developmental milestones and signs of atypical development, in addition to knowledge of local and state resources for connecting families with evaluation or diagnostic services and available interventions or supports for the child. Practical tips for assessment and evaluation of developmental delays include: (a) clarifying the purpose of the developmental assessment, (b) gathering information from multiple sources using multiple assessment methods, (c) considering relevant cultural and linguistic issues, and (d) gathering information that can inform intervention, including a child's strengths. Considerations for including children with developmental disabilities in early childhood education programs involve promoting a culture of inclusion, providing professional development and training to staff, and integrating inclusion into a multitier system of supports.

8

Family Engagement
in Early Childhood Education

Effectively engaging families is critical to the success of early childhood education programs and to promoting positive early academic outcomes for young children. This chapter will review research related to family engagement in early childhood education and offer strategies for strengthening partnerships between schools and families. In addition, conjoint/collaborative behavioral consultation will be discussed as a framework for bringing educators and families together to meet the needs of individual children with the context of a multitier system of support. A case example will be provided to illustrate how this framework can be applied to early childhood education programs.

Family Engagement

Many models of family–school relations have emerged in the education literature. Some have focused on methods for increasing parents' involvement in school activities while others have emphasized schools' roles in reaching out to families in support of students' academic outcomes. Halgunseth, Peterson, Stark, and Moodie (2009, p. 3) have offered the following comprehensive conceptual model of family engagement in early childhood education programs centered on six factors:

1. Early childhood education programs encourage and validate family participation in decision making related to their children's education. Families should act as advocates for their children and early childhood education program by actively taking part in decision making opportunities.

2. Consistent, two-way communication is facilitated through multiple forms and is responsive to the linguistic preference of the family. Communication should be both school and family initiated and should be timely and continuous, inviting conversations about both the child's educational experience as well as the larger program.

3. Families and early childhood education programs collaborate and exchange knowledge. Family members share their unique knowledge and skills through volunteering and actively engaging in events and activities at schools. Teachers seek out information about their students' lives, families, and communities and integrate this information into their curriculum and instructional practices.

4. Early childhood education programs and families place an emphasis on creating and sustaining learning activities at home and in the community that extend the teachings of the program so as to enhance each child's early learning.

5. Families create a home environment that values learning and supports programs. Families and programs collaborate in establishing goals for children both at home and at school.

6. Early childhood education programs create an ongoing and comprehensive system for promoting family engagement by ensuring that program leadership and teachers are dedicated, trained, and receive the supports they need to fully engage families.

This model assumes that all families are *involved* in their children's learning and well-being but that early childhood education programs must engage families to work together on behalf of children. Research has shown that strong family–school partnerships are associated with greater academic motivation, grade promotion, and socioemotional skills for children from diverse backgrounds (Halgunseth et al., 2009). This model of family engagement will be used as a framework for the strategies and practical considerations offered in this chapter, following a review of research on family engagement in early childhood education programs.

Research on Family Engagement in Early Childhood Education Programs

Until recently the research evidence related to family involvement at school during the early childhood years and children's school readiness outcomes had been somewhat limited, although research support existed for strategies that target families' support of young children's preacademic skill development (Boethl, 2004). For example, in their sample of predominately African American, urban Head Start students, Fantuzzo, McWayne, Perry, and Childs (2004) found that home-based parent involvement activities were positively associated with children's approaches to learning and receptive vocabulary, and negatively associated with problem behaviors in the classroom. In this particular study, home-based involvement was found to have stronger associations with positive outcomes for young children than school-based involvement. More recently, a growing body of evidence suggests that family engagement can positively influence young children's early learning outcomes. In particular, the Getting Ready intervention, an approach that integrates professional consultation models to promote parent engagement and collaborative parent–teacher partnerships in early childhood education programs, has demonstrated positive effects on young children's social-emotional, language, and early literacy skills (Sheridan, Knoche, Edwards, Bovaird, & Kupzyk, 2010; Sheridan, Knoche, Kupzyk, Edwards, & Marvin, 2011). One of these professional consultation models, collaborative/conjoint consultation, will be discussed in more detail later in this chapter.

Research has also shown that three primary family involvement processes promote positive outcomes for young children: (a) parenting, (b) home–school relationships, and (c) responsibility for learning outcomes (Weiss, Caspe, & Lopez, 2006). In the area of parenting, early parent–child relationships that are nurturing, warm, and responsive are associated with positive learning outcomes for young children (Weiss et al., 2006). Emotional support from parents/primary caregivers, cognitive stimulation at home, and complex language exposure are also associated with young children's academic success (Weiss, Bouffard, Bridglall, & Gordon, 2009). In the area of home–school relationships, parent participation in preschool-based activities and regular communication between families and teachers have been shown to be associated with positive learning outcomes (Arnold, Zeljo, Doctoroff, & Ortiz, 2008; Weiss, Caspe, & Lopez, 2006), and outreach from school and community leaders is associated with higher levels of family involvement (Weiss, Bouffard, et al., 2009). Parent involvement in school-based activities and home–school conferencing is also related to parents' satisfaction with their level of contact with early childhood education personnel (McWayne, Campos, & Owsianik, 2008). Research has shown that low-income families face more logistical barriers to involvement in school programs, such as access to transportation and job-related scheduling conflicts (Weiss, Bouffard, et al., 2009). Parent and child gender, maternal education, and linguistic background have been found to be associated with parent involvement in Head Start programming (McWayne et al., 2008). In the area of shared responsibility for learning outcomes, reading to young children at home and showing them how to write words are examples of strategies that have been linked to their acquisition of better early literacy and language skills (Weiss, Caspe, & Lopez, 2006). There is also some research support for the effectiveness of parent-training strategies that focus on developing young children's early literacy and mathematical skills (Boethl, 2004).

More research is needed to better understand the complex relationships among family and child characteristics, family involvement in early childhood education programs, and children's outcomes. Further research is also necessary regarding how best to engage families to support their children's success in early childhood education and beyond. Based on the available research, however, Boethl (2004) recommends that early childhood education programs help families provide learning resources and experiences for their young children (e.g., providing books and other literacy materials for families, offering trainings and increasing awareness of the benefits of reading to young children, and offering activities that families can do at home with their children). Encouraging families to remain involved in their children's schooling after the transition from preschool to kindergarten is also important, as research has shown that parents' at-school involvement decreases when their children begin kindergarten (Boethl, 2004).

Strategies for Strengthening Family–School Partnerships to Promote Family Engagement

Organized by the six factors within Halgunseth and colleagues' (2009) model of family engagement, the following strategies and practical considerations, which are summarized on the companion website, are intended to provide an overview of general approaches and issues related to promoting family engagement in early childhood education programs. It is not intended to be an exhaustive list, and it is recognized that some of these strategies may not be applicable to all early childhood education settings nor appropriate for all families. The *Early Childhood Education* companion website includes a list of resources for further exploring strategies for strengthening family–school partnerships.

Encourage and Validate Family Participation in Decision Making

Create a Welcoming Environment for Families. To encourage family participation in educational decision making, families must first feel welcome in the early childhood education setting. Developing a welcoming environment includes considerations such as paying attention to the way classrooms are decorated and organized, how families and students are greeted by staff members, and creating a family reception area that is warm and inviting (Prior & Gerard, 2007). This also includes making sure that families' cultural and linguistic backgrounds, as well as diverse family structures, are represented and appreciated in the school environment (Halgunseth et al., 2009; Prior & Gerard, 2007).

Offer Ample Opportunities for Families to Participate in Decision Making. Family participation in educational decision making can range from providing input into the curriculum, school activities, and food choices offered; being a member of the early childhood program's board of directors or policy committee; to developing individual educational goals for their child in collaboration with the child's teacher.

Facilitate Consistent, Two-Way Communication

Consider the Purpose of the Communication and Family Preferences when Selecting a Communication Method. Knopf and Swick (2008) provide a detailed discussion and summary of the purposes, strengths, and weaknesses of common family communication strategies utilized by early childhood education programs. For example, home visits can be used to learn about the home context or to provide services to a family and are typically implemented with a low- to medium-level frequency. The authors point out that the strengths of home visits include seeing the child and family in context and meeting with the family in their comfort zone, but a weakness of this communication method is that it may be perceived by some families as too invasive. Use of e-mail for communicating with families, on the other hand, can be done with high frequency and provides immediate written communication that can be translated into different languages (Knopf & Swick, 2008). As the authors note, a weakness of this form of communication, however, is that some families may not have access to e-mail. Early childhood education professionals should consider these factors when deciding which communication strategies are most appropriate for meeting the needs of the family and the purpose of the communication in a particular instance (Knopf & Swick, 2008). Other strategies for establishing communication with families include program handbooks, enrollment interviews, daily notebooks or record forms, newsletters, activity calendars, phone calls and phone trees, back-to-school or family nights, and family–school conferences (Prior & Gerard, 2007).

Be Receptive to Families' Communication Efforts. Part of facilitating two-way communication is recognizing when families are attempting to communicate with school staff about their child and being receptive to these communication attempts. This may mean teachers being available to talk briefly with parents during drop-off and pick-up times and responding promptly to phone calls, e-mails, or notes from parents. It also involves being receptive to families' individual or cultural preferences for communication methods (Halgunseth et al., 2009). Conveying warmth, genuineness, and trustworthiness, as well as using strategies such as demonstrating empathy and positive regard, have been found to be components of effective helping relationships (McGivern, Ray-Subramanian, & Auster, 2008) and may help promote meaningful reciprocal communication between educators and families.

Collaborate and Exchange Knowledge

Offer a Variety of Opportunities for Family Engagement. Knopf and Swick (2008) note the need to "provide families with many different pathways to be involved" (p. 425) and get parent input into methods of involvement that are most useful to them. These opportunities can include involvement in school-based activities or involvement in home-based learning activities (Prior & Gerard, 2007).

Gather Information from Families to Integrate into the Classroom. Families can also teach school staff and other students about their cultures, communities, and experiences. Educators can gather information, as appropriate, from families to incorporate into instructional activities and to support the learning of individual children. It is important to recognize that families are an important source of knowledge regarding their child's development and learning (Halgunseth et al., 2009).

Create and Sustain Learning Activities at Home and in the Community

Offer Resources for Supporting Home-Based Learning Activities. Early childhood education professionals can provide families with ideas for home-based learning activities, such as reading to children, storytelling, counting games, and art projects (Prior & Gerard, 2007). Early childhood education programs can also create lending libraries for families to borrow learning materials to use at home (Prior & Gerard, 2007). The *Early Childhood Education* companion website includes a list of resources for families to support young children's learning.

Establish Partnerships with Community Organizations to Support Children's Learning Outside of School. Partnering with community organizations to support young children's learning can involve helping link families to resources in their communities by holding program events at libraries, zoos, museums, and other community gathering places (Weiss, Caspe, & Lopez, 2006). Parent meetings or parent–teacher conferences can also be held in off-site community locations to foster connections with the larger community (Halgunseth et al., 2009). Additionally, early childhood education programs can assist with connecting families to meaningful support networks and peer-to-peer groups (Office for Head Start, 2011). School–community partnership activities can take many forms and can be student-centered (e.g., tutoring), family-centered (e.g., adult education programs), school-centered (e.g., donation of equipment), or community-centered (e.g., outreach programs; Eagle, Dowd-Eagle, & Sheridan, 2008).

Promote Home Environments that Value and Support Learning

Provide Families with Information Regarding the Importance of Home-Based Learning Activities. In addition to offering material resources to support home-based learning, early childhood education professionals can help promote home environments that value learning by informing families of the importance of home-based learning and the benefits of reading to young children at home (Boethl, 2004; Halgunseth et al., 2009). Programs can also offer parent workshops and parent–child groups to promote warm and nurturing parenting (Weiss, Caspe, & Lopez, 2006), which serves as a foundation for positive learning outcomes.

Collaborate with Families to Develop Educational Goals. Families should be encouraged to participate in developing educational goals for their children in collaboration with early childhood education program staff. These goals can focus on learning at school and at home (Halgunseth et al., 2009). Promoting home environments that value and support learning can also include supporting parents in reaching their own educational and training goals (Office for Head Start, 2011).

Create an Ongoing and Comprehensive System for Promoting Family Engagement

Integrate Family Engagement into a Multitier System of Supports. Family engagement can be integrated into each tier within a multitier system of supports. Most of the strategies discussed in this chapter are intended to be implemented at the universal level to support the learning of all students. For students who require additional supports to promote their academic and behavioral development, parents should be involved in the process of determining which additional supports are needed for their child.

Provide Ongoing Professional Development for Staff Regarding Family Engagement. Creating and sustaining a comprehensive system for promoting family engagement within early childhood education requires a commitment to ongoing professional development. Example areas for professional development related to family engagement include developing knowledge regarding communication styles and relationship building, learning about different kinds of education and training opportunities available to families, and strategies for enhancing parent–child relationships and encouraging parent leadership and advocacy (Office for Head Start, 2011).

Addressing Barriers to Family-School Partnerships

Barriers to effective family–school partnerships exist for families, educators, and the family–school relationship (Christenson, 2004). Christenson (2004) explains that these can take the form of both structural and psychological barriers and offers examples of each. For families, structural barriers can include child care and transportation needs or economic, emotional, or time constraints. Examples of psychological barriers for families are perceived lack of responsiveness to parental needs or linguistic or cultural differences that influence knowledge of school policies and practices. For educators, structural barriers can include time constraints and lack of funding for family outreach programs. Examples of psychological barriers include feeling wary about interacting with families or fear of conflict. Christenson (2004) lists lack of routine communication systems among examples of structural barriers for the family–school relationship. Psychological barriers include limited use of perspective taking or empathizing with each other.

These barriers can be addressed through adoption and demonstration of constructivist attitudes; an atmosphere of "trust, effective communication, and a mutual problem-solving orientation" (p. 95); and actions focused on building shared responsibility for children's learning (Christenson, 2004). Constructivist attitudes can be demonstrated by families and educators by: (a) listening to one another's perspective; (b) viewing differences as strengths; (c) focusing on mutual interests; (d) sharing information to coconstruct understandings and interventions; (e) respecting each other's skills and knowledge by asking for ideas and opinions; (f) planning and making decisions together that address parents', teachers', and students' needs; (g) sharing in decision making about a child's educational program; (h) sharing resources to work toward goal attainment; (i) providing a common message about schoolwork and behavior; (j) demonstrating a willingness to address conflict; (k) refraining from finding fault; and (l) committing to share resources (Christenson, 2004). An atmosphere that promotes trust, effective communication, and mutual problem-solving can be developed by creating a school climate that is welcoming and inclusive for all families, informing families about school policies and practices, and involving parents in assessment and intervention processes. Actions for building shared responsibility between families and educators include (a) garnering administrative support; (b) advocating at a systems level; (c) implementing family–school teams; (d) increasing problem solving across home and school; (e) identifying and managing conflict; (f) supporting families; (g) helping teachers improve communication and relationships with families; and (h) collaborating with others in developing cohesive, coordinated family-school-community interventions (Christenson, 2004).

Conjoint/Collaborative Behavioral Consultation

One framework for bringing educators and families together to meet the needs of individual children with the context of a multitier system of support is conjoint/collaborative behavioral consultation. Sheridan and Kratochwill

(2010) define conjoint behavioral consultation (CBC) as "a strength-based, cross-system problem-solving and decision-making model wherein parents, teachers, and other caregivers or service providers work as partners and share responsibility for promoting positive and consistent outcomes related to a child's academic, behavioral, and social-emotional development" (p. 25). This process is facilitated by a consultant, such as a school psychologist, who works collaboratively with parents, teachers, and other school staff (Sheridan, Clarke, Knoche, & Edwards, 2006). The overarching goals of CBC involve promoting positive outcomes for children, promoting parent engagement, and establishing and strengthening home–school partnerships. This model of service delivery is applicable to multiple settings including early childhood education programs. CBC is uniquely suited to be incorporated into multitier systems of support and offers a method for integrating parents into the problem-solving process at various levels of intervention (Sheridan & Kratochwill, 2010). This section provides an overview of CBC and its application to early childhood education; readers are referred to Sheridan and Kratochwill (2010) for a detailed presentation of the procedural characteristics and range of applications of CBC.

In their framework for CBC within the context of promoting family–school connections, Sheridan and Kratochwill (2010) note that effective home–school partnerships, "(a) are collaborative and interdependent and (b) embrace shared responsibility for educating and socializing children" (p. 2). The theoretical foundations for their framework draw from ecological theory, behavioral theory, and a family-centered approach. From an ecological perspective, children develop within multiple systems, environments, and contexts and are affected by the interactions and interconnections among them, such as family–school relationships. Behavioral theory focuses on observable, learned behavior, environmental factors that influence behavior, and objective documentation of intervention effects. A family-centered perspective promotes family empowerment, developing skills and competencies, building on existing family strengths, and strengthening social supports to address family-identified needs. This perspective has been extended to a partnership-centered approach that includes empowering both families and educators and building on their combined strengths to develop new skills and competencies to address jointly determined needs (Sheridan & Kratochwill, 2010).

CBC consists of four stages: (a) conjoint needs/problem identification, (b) conjoint needs/problem analysis, (c) plan implementation, and (d) conjoint plan evaluation (Sheridan & Kratochwill, 2010). The needs identification stages involves identifying the strengths of the child, family, teacher, and systems; behaviorally defining and prioritizing needs; and establishing baseline data collection procedures. The needs analysis stage consists of evaluating the baseline data, selecting behavioral goals for the child, considering environmental influences on the child's behavior, and collaboratively developing an intervention plan. The plan implementation stage is the phase during which the intervention procedures are employed across settings. Finally, the plan evaluation stage involves examining the behavioral data collected to assess the effects of the intervention.

CBC has been implemented successfully in early childhood education settings. In a study examining the effects of CBC in early childhood populations, Sheridan, Clarke, et al. (2006) found that it led to significant improvements in parents' perceptions of their communication with their child's teacher. The researchers also found that parents and teachers reported high levels of acceptability, satisfaction, and goal attainment with CBC (Sheridan, Clarke, et al., 2006). Sheridan and colleagues have also incorporated strategies based on CBC into a parent engagement intervention (i.e., Getting Ready intervention) intended to facilitate school readiness among disadvantaged preschool children (Sheridan, Knoche, Kupzyk, et al., 2011). The Getting Ready intervention integrates triadic (i.e., parent-child-professional) and conjoint/collaborative (i.e., family-school) consultation strategies. The triadic strategies involve promoting warm, supportive parent–child interactions; affirming parents' competence; focusing parents' attention on child development; providing developmental information; and modeling or suggesting strategies parents can use to support their child's learning (Sheridan, Knoche, Edwards, et al., 2010). The conjoint/collaborative strategies involve identifying the child's strengths, establishing learning goals, assessing the child's current levels of performance, creating plans to support the child's growth, and monitoring the child's progress (Sheridan, Knoche, Edwards, et al., 2010). The Getting Ready intervention has been shown to improve preschool children's language and early literacy skills and social emotional competencies (Sheridan, Knoche, Edwards, et al., 2010; Sheridan, Knoche, Kupzyk, et al., 2011).

CBC Case Example. Gabriela is a 4-year-old girl attending a prekindergarten program at Spruce Pine Elementary School. She lives with her parents, 2-year-old brother, and paternal grandmother. Gabriela was born in the United States but her parents are originally from Guatemala, and Spanish is the primary language spoken in their home. Gabriela is fluent in speaking and understanding both English and Spanish. Her pre-K teacher, Ms. Williams, has observed that Gabriela has strengths in her letter- and number-identification skills but is having some difficulty with transitioning between activities in the classroom. Ms. Williams had been communicating with Gabriela's family through brief, informal conversations during drop-off and pick-up times and periodic notes home—which were translated into Spanish—that highlighted Gabriela's strengths and early academic skill development. Ms. Williams mentioned in one of the notes that she had some concerns about Gabriela's difficulty with transitioning between activities in the classroom and that it was becoming disruptive to the class. Ms. Williams asked if Gabriela's parents could meet with her to discuss these concerns and that she would like to have the school psychologist, Ms. Levy, who is bilingual in English and Spanish, join them. Gabriela's mother called Ms. Williams and said that both she and Gabriela's father would like to be involved in the discussion but that he has limited availability due to his work schedule. They agreed upon a time that worked for Ms. Williams, Ms. Levy, and Gabriela's parents and decided to meet at the family's home.

Conjoint Needs Identification. During the initial conjoint needs identification interview, Ms. Williams stated that she would like to see Gabriela better follow instructions related to cleaning up materials, lining up by the classroom door, and moving from one activity to another. Gabriela's parents reported that they do not have any concerns about her at home but that she can sometimes be stubborn. The team identified some of Gabriela's strengths, such as her self-confidence and her letter- and number-identification skills. Identified strengths of her family included her supportive parents and grandmother, her exposure to two languages at home, and the frequent reading that her grandmother does with Gabriela. Ms. Levy helped identify strengths of Ms. Williams and her classroom, such as high expectations for all students and 10 years of experience teaching young children. Together, the team agreed upon a goal of increasing Gabriela's compliance with instructions to transition between activities and established an operational definition of the target behavior. Ms. Levy agreed to collect baseline data through direct observation of Gabriela in the classroom over the next week.

Conjoint Needs Analysis. One week later, Gabriela's parents, her teacher, and the school psychologist met at school to review the observational data that

Ms. Levy had collected. The data showed that Gabriela was following teacher instructions to transition to a new activity 40% of the time. It appeared that Gabriela seemed to transition promptly to the next activity during predictable daily routines, such as hanging her coat up when she arrives in the classroom and getting out a toy to play with, or going over to the rug for circle time during which Ms. Williams read to the class and presented the "letter of the week." Her parents reported that Gabriela loves learning about letters and often tells them which letter she is learning about in school that week. The team discussed possible strategies and created an intervention plan for helping Gabriela to transition promptly between activities.

Plan Implementation. At the classroom level, Ms. Williams began to verbally foreshadow transitions more systematically throughout the day and placed a visual picture schedule on the wall to which she would refer when giving verbal instructions. At the individual level, she made Gabriela her own picture schedule to color and use as a reference. Gabriela's parents posted a picture schedule for her bedtime routine in Gabriela's bedroom to help reinforce the practice of anticipating transitions and following a sequence of activities. Ms. Williams also moved circle time to the end of each morning and told Gabriela that she could help introduce the letter of the week, and tell the class how to say the name of the letter in Spanish, if she followed her picture schedule that day. Ms. Levy conducted brief observations in the classroom twice per week to collect data on Gabriela's compliance with transitioning between activities.

Conjoint Plan Evaluation. Ms. Williams, Ms. Levy, and Gabriela's parents met one month later at the family's home to evaluate the outcomes of their conjoint intervention plan. The observational data collected by Ms. Levy indicated that Gabriela's rate of compliance with teacher instructions for transitioning between activities increased from 40% to 80% and Ms. Williams reported that Gabriela seemed to enjoy helping with circle time at the end of each morning. Her parents were pleased that Gabriela's teacher has noticed improvements and they reported that Gabriela seems to enjoy using her bedtime visual schedule at home and reviewing the letter of the week at home with her grandmother in Spanish. The team decided to continue implementing the intervention strategies and maintain frequent contact regarding Gabriela's progress through phone calls, which her parents had indicated during the consultation process was their preferred method of communication.

Summary

Family engagement is an important component of early childhood education. Research has shown that home-based parent involvement activities are positively associated with learning outcomes (Boethl, 2004; Fantuzzo et al., 2004) and professional consultation models that promote parent engagement and collaborative parent–teacher partnerships have been found to have positive effects on young children's social-emotional, language, and early literacy skills (Sheridan, Knoche, Edwards, et al., 2010; Sheridan, Knoche, Kupzyk, et al., 2011). Researchers have found that parenting, home–school relationships, and shared responsibility for learning outcomes are the three primary family involvement processes that promote positive outcomes for young children (Weiss, Caspe, & Lopez, 2006). Based on Halgunseth and colleagues' (2009) model of family engagement, six general strategies can be implemented to strengthen partnerships between families and early childhood education programs: (a) encourage and validate family participation in decision making; (b) facilitate consistent, two-way communication; (c) collaborate and exchange knowledge; (d) create and sustain learning activities at home and in the community; (e) promote home environments that value and support learning; and (f) create an ongoing and comprehensive system for promoting family engagement. Conjoint/collaborative consultation is an example of a framework for promoting family–school partnerships within a multitier system of support to address the needs of an individual child, in addition to the many strategies that can be implemented at the universal level.

9

Summary and Future Directions
for Early Childhood MTSS

The development of multitiered systems of supports (MTSS) for the early childhood setting is a major milestone for early childhood education. Surveys indicate that state-level directors and coordinators of early childhood education indicate various levels of implementation from preliminary discussion to full implementation (Linas, Carta, & Greenwood, 2010; Linas, Greenwood, & Carta, 2009). Ultimately, states and early childhood centers will need to address the unique needs of their young learners because no one model of MTSS will likely be sufficient or necessary for all children and families. Implementing MTSS within early childhood settings should be undertaken in a thoughtful, well-planned manner.

Considerations in Implementing MTSS

Several key areas should be considered to effectively implement the various levels of services involved in MTSS. Some key factors identified include leadership, assessment and data management, culture and beliefs, professional development, staff recruitment, and resource allocation (O'Connor & Freeman, 2012).

Commitment from leadership is essential in making systems level changes. Leaders within early childhood settings will need to understand the principles and practices involved within MTSS. Adoption of an organizational framework provides a clear guide outlining how to build a consensus with key stakeholders (teachers, support personnel, parents, other agencies, etc.). Second, the need for clear structures becomes apparent. Early childhood personnel and leaders ideally meet, possibly two to four times throughout the year, to review and discuss research evidence and evaluate data to monitor goals of their program. Development of specific routines and processes ensures that all individuals understand expectations and roles.

Successful implementation of MTSS relies on the effective collection and appropriate analysis of data. Assessments should be chosen carefully so that they are psychometrically sound and evidence-based for measuring key academic, behavioral, and social-emotional skills. Decisions can only be as good as the data upon which they are based. Agencies should devote time to train individuals to provide support for all staff. This may involve one central individual to manage all data and provide summary reports related to agency goals, while multiple "coaches" are available to coordinate and carry out activities of collecting data.

Another key consideration involves the culture and beliefs that exist within a district or agency. These factors may have a strong influence on staff and students. Attitudes such as believing that teachers can effectively teach all children influence commitments to MTSS. O'Connor and Freeman (2012) recommend providing opportunities for open dialogue. Perhaps offering teachers the chance to anonymously record the percent of students they believe can achieve grade-level or age-appropriate learning and behavior goals. For those individuals who do not believe 100% of children can be successful, there is a need for them to process those biases and perceived challenges. Employing powerful examples from other schools, or possibly within the district or agency, can begin to change perceptions. Viewing MTSS as a current fad in education or words without action doom it to failure.

Along with culture and beliefs, the recruitment and selection of top staff directly impacts an effective MTSS process. Some preservice training programs may not adequately prepare individuals with regard to MTSS concepts or skills. Districts and agencies will need to supplement training of individuals without requisite skills; alternatively, it may be advantageous to partner with local universities and training programs to discuss the unique needs and skills necessary for early childhood personnel. Those involved in the hiring process should incorporate relevant skills-based questions to identify those individuals who can contribute to leadership and implementation of MTSS.

Finally, districts and agencies must be aware of the resources necessary to support the various initiatives central to MTSS. While finances dominate conversations in education, allocations of staff roles and time must be determined as well. Ideally, MTSS will provide optimal use of staff in identifying the most effective programs based on data, allowing districts and agencies to discard outdated, ineffective practices. These changes to staff roles and time may initially cause some hesitation, but may be avoided by ensuring that all individuals are committed to the mission and goals of MTSS.

Developing an effective, sustainable MTSS should be viewed as a process, and not "all-or-nothing." Ball and Trammell (2011) recommend that full-scale implementation of MTSS within the preschool setting may be premature at this time because of lack of the necessary resources and expertise from external research partnerships. A more realistic goal in working toward full implementation at this time may be to focus on universal screening and

TABLE 9.1 Sample Four-Year Implementation Plan for Pre-K MTSS

Year 1
- Build consensus with key stakeholders regarding legal precedents for MTSS.
- Educate key stakeholders about core components of MTSS.
- Establish and implement a measurement system to track student performance, family involvement, and implementation fidelity.
- Identify and train a team of core experts for data collection, analysis, decision making, and troubleshooting.
- Train teams on screeners, progress monitoring measures, and other assessments, as well as how to interpret data, goal setting, graphing, and data-based decision making.
- Conduct universal screenings and benchmark assessments.
- Identify school leaders or experts to assist with data collection, management, interpretation, decision making, and troubleshooting.

Year 2
- Provide professional development opportunities on implementing effective academic, social-emotional, and behavioral curricula.
- Identify supplemental interventions and provide training.
- Continue implementing measurement systems from Year 1 with assistance from the team of experts.
- Identify or establish a problem-solving team in each school to participate in Year 3 training; identify team facilitators to attend training on the problem-solving model.

Year 3
- Begin implementing tiered intervention services.
- Provide training to problem-solving teams on the problem-solving model.
- Provide coaching for problem-solving teams.
- Continue implementing measurement system from Year 1.
- Determine eligibility procedures for Year 4.

Year 4
- Continue implementing measurement system from Year 1.
- Problem-solving teams should meet regularly to determine entitlement decisions with coaching.
- Consider networking meetings for team facilitators and coaches on a monthly basis.
- Conduct a needs assessment to determine areas of strength and weakness within the MTSS.

Adapted from Burns & Gibbons (2008).

ensure an appropriate general curriculum with opportunities for delivering more intensive interventions and supports. Additionally, the need for continuous professional development is highlighted, furthering teachers' knowledge and skills. Team members should consider developing various systems in phases over several years (possibly 4 to 5 years). An excellent 4-year implementation plan was offered by Burns and Gibbons (2008) and is adapted below for pre-K settings.

The Future of MTSS

Comparatively, the science of creating tiered services to address the needs of young children is still in its early development. Practitioners and researchers will need to work together over the coming years to further define what practices constitute appropriate MTSS, realizing that what works for one district or agency may not be right for another. The following areas represent critical research agendas and issues for developing early childhood MTSS.

Lack of Access to Early Childhood Education. Not all children in the United States have access to early childhood education despite the advantages to later education (Heckman, 2000). At times, children may attend programs offered through local school districts, Head Start programs, or community-based programs (private or parochial schools). Advocacy in policy and legislation is needed to relate the importance of early education to promoting developmental skills necessary for later educational success.

Comprehensive Training for All Stakeholders in Early Childhood MTSS. As noted previously, training is important for all involved in MTSS, including administrators, teachers, support personnel, and parents. Typically, there are fewer requirements for teachers in early childhood settings compared to the K-12 setting. In addition, there is typically lower compensation, which may lead to a higher turnover rate for early childhood educators. Recruitment and retention of top early educators is crucial for early childhood education's success. It is important to recognize the need for continuous professional development of early educators. Resources related to professional development from the RTI Action Network (www.rtinetwork.org) provide a starting point to address the unique strengths and needs of settings.

Ensuring High Quality Data Collection and Analysis. Integral to the functioning of MTSS is the collection and analysis of data. Districts and agencies must grapple with identifying the tools useful in collecting data to meet their outlined goals. Personnel must be well trained to collect this data with fidelity and knowledgeable in interpreting the data.

Comparison of Screeners and Progress Monitoring Tools. Given the issue above, more research is needed in comparing the various screeners and progress monitoring tools mentioned throughout this book. Comparisons based on the reliability, validity, cost effectiveness, and feasibility are needed. Without this information, MTSS will struggle to meet children's needs.

Research-Based Curricula and Interventions at Various Tiers. Much more research is needed to investigate evidence-based curricula and interventions for early childhood populations. In a review of 14 preschool curriculums, only 2 of the 14 had impact on student-level outcomes (Russell et al., 2007). The What Works Clearinghouse (www.ies.ed.gov/ncee/wwc/) provides current information related to positive outcomes for numerous preschool curricula in a variety of early childhood education outcomes (e.g., early reading, phonological processing, oral language, and social outcomes), few of which have evidenced positive outcomes. In addition, there is a lack of translating manualized interventions for implementation in the early childhood classroom. These interventions must be shared by education specialists with classroom teachers and they should span all developmental domains—academic, physical, social-emotional, and behavioral. Additionally, there must be a commitment on the parts of researchers and practitioners to work in tandem, with researchers sharing feedback about the efficacy of well-controlled intervention studies in clinical trials and practitioners relaying the effectiveness of those interventions in the "real world."

Cost, Feasibility, and Sustainability. Innovation in instructional and service delivery models will lead to changes in the cost of providing educational services to children. This may mean hiring or contracting additional specialists or experts, investing in manualized interventions or specialized equipment, or purchasing new screening and diagnostic instruments. Administrators will be challenged to arrange all the pieces necessary to provide a high quality early childhood education. To this end, administrators may wish to consult and share ways in which they have funded and allocated financial and personnel resources to meet the needs of children and families. This may also necessitate working to address needed policies and legislative initiatives at the state and federal levels. Another challenge related to cost, feasibility, and sustainability is the current provision of early childhood education. Given the various agencies involved (e.g., districts, private/parochial schools, federally funded programs), there will be unique challenges in coordinating services and meeting mandated standards from the various program sponsors.

Outcome Data for Students, Especially Those From Culturally and Linguistically Diverse Backgrounds. Ultimately, data supporting the improved outcomes of children will determine the success of MTSS. As emphasized by No Child Left Behind (2001), educators in the K-12 schools must document the progress of culturally and linguistically diverse students (i.e., major racial and ethnic groups, English language learners) as well as students with disabilities and those from low-income backgrounds. Moving forward, outcome data from students in these groups should be monitored closely.

Summary

Though still in its early formation, MTSS has grown in conceptualization and implementation across the United States. With the potential benefits of providing key early academic, social-emotional, behavioral, and physical experiences to prevent or remediate developmental delays and disabilities, MTSS will continue to take center stage in early childhood education discussions. Given the current accomplishments and research, early childhood MTSS has a promising future.

References

Achenbach, T. M., & Rescorla, L. A. (2000). *Manual for ASEBA preschool forms and profiles.* Burlington, VT: University of Vermont, Research Center for Children, Youth, & Families.

American Academy of Pediatrics. (2004). *Caring for your baby and young child: Birth to age 5.* New York: Bantam Books.

American Educational Research Association (AERA), American Psychological Association (APA), & National Council on Measurement in Education (NCME). (1999). *Standards for educational and psychological testing.* Washington, DC: AERA.

American Psychiatric Association. (2000). *Diagnostic and statistical manual of mental disorders* (4th ed., text rev.). Washington, DC: Author.

American Psychological Association, Presidential Task Force on Evidence-Based Practice (2006). Evidence-based practice in psychology. *American Psychologist, 61*(4), 271–285. doi:10.1037/0003-066X.61.4.271

American Speech-Language-Hearing Association. (n.d.). *How does your child hear and talk?* Retrieved from http://www.asha.org/public/speech/development/chart.htm

Anderson, L. M., Shinn, C., Fullilove, M. T., Scrimshaw, S. C., Fielding, J. E., Normand, J., … Task Force on Community Preventive Services. (2003). The effectiveness of early childhood development programs: A systematic review. *American Journal of Preventive Medicine, 24*(3S), 32–46. doi:10.1016/S0749-3797(02)00655-4

Arnold, D. H., Zeljo, A., Doctoroff, G. L., & Ortiz, C. (2008). Parent involvement in preschool: Predictors and the relation of involvement to preliteracy development. *School Psychology Review, 37,* 74–90.

Ball, C. R., & Trammell, B. A. (2011). Response-to-intervention in high-risk preschools: Critical issues for implementation. *Psychology in the Schools, 48*(5), 502–512. doi:10.1002/pits.20572

Benedict, E. A., Horner, R. H., & Squires, J. K. (2007). Assessment and implementation of positive behavior support in preschools. *Topics in Early Childhood Special Education, 27,* 174–192.

Boethel, M. (2004). *Readiness: School, family, and community connections.* Austin, TX: National Center for Family and Community Connections with Schools, Southwest Educational Development Laboratory. Retrieved from http://www.sedl.org/pubs/catalog/items/fam37.html

Bradfield, T., Wackerle-Holman, A., & McConnell, S. (2011, September). *Using IGDIs to identify children for tiered intervention.* Santa Ana Pueblo, NM: Center for Response to Intervention in Early Childhood, University of Kansas. Retrieved from http://www.crtiec.org/rti_summit/2010/2011RTISummit.shtml

Brassard, M. R., & Boehm, A. E. (2007). *Preschool assessment: Principles and practices.* New York: Guilford.

Brown, M., & Tom, K. (2012, February). *Addressing social emotional learning through RTI in early childhood settings.* Paper presented at the annual convention of The National Association of School Psychologists, Philadelphia, PA.

Bruns, D. A., & Mogharreban, C. C. (2007). The gap between beliefs and practices: Early childhood practitioners' perceptions about inclusion. *Journal of Research in Childhood Education, 21,* 229–241.

Burns, M. K., & Gibbons, K. A. (2008). *Implementing response-to-intervention in elementary and secondary schools: Procedures to assure scientific-based practices.* New York: Routledge.

Burns, M. K., & Gibbons, K. (2012). *Implementing response-to-intervention in elementary and secondary schools: Procedures to assure scientific-based practices* (2nd ed.). New York: Routledge.

Buysee, V., & Peisner-Feinberg, E. (2010). Recognition and response: Response to intervention for prek. *Young Exceptional Children, 13*(4), 2–13.

Carta, J. J., & Kong, N. Y. (2007). Trends and issues in interventions for preschoolers with disabilities. In S. Odom, R. Horner, M. Snell, & J. Blacher (Eds.), *Handbook of developmental disabilities* (pp. 181–198). New York: Guilford.

Center for Response to Intervention in Early Childhood. (2012). Retrieved from http://www.crtiec.org.

Children's Learning Institute. (2009*). C-PALLS+ The CIRCLE phonological awareness, language, and literacy system+* (Technical manual). Houston, TX: Author.

Christenson, S. L. (2004). The family-school partnership: An opportunity to promote the learning competence of all students. *School Psychology Review, 33,* 83–104.

Cloud, N. (2002). Culturally and linguistically responsive instructional planning. In A. Artiles & A. Ortiz (Eds.), *English language learners with special education needs: Identification, assessment, and instruction* (pp. 107–132). Washington, DC: Center for Applied Linguistics and Delta Systems.

Cohen, N. J., Davine, M., Horodezky, N., Lipsett, L., & Isaacson, L. (1993). Unsuspected language impairment in psychiatrically disturbed children: Prevalence and language and behavioral characteristics. *Journal of the American Academy of Child and Adolescent Psychiatry, 32*(3), 595–603.

Coleman, M. R., Buysse, V., & Neitzel, J. (2006). *Recognition and response: An early intervening system for young children at-risk for learning disabilities. Full report.* Chapel Hill: The University of North Carolina at Chapel Hill, FPG Child Development Institute.

Colorado Department of Education. (2008). *Response to intervention: A practitioner's guide to implementation.* Denver, CO: Author.

Council for Exceptional Children (CEC). (2008). *Classifying the state of evidence for special education professional practices: CEC practice study manual.* Arlington, VA: Author.

Deno, S. L. (1985). Curriculum-based measurement: The emerging alternative. *Exceptional Children, 52,* 219–232.

DiPerna, J. C., & Morgan, P. (2005). *EARLI project literacy probes, form A.* Unpublished assessment.

Division for Early Childhood (DEC) & National Association for the Education of Young Children (NAEYC). (2009). *Early childhood inclusion: A joint position statement of the Division for Early Childhood (DEC) and the National Association for the Education of Young Children (NAEYC).* Chapel Hill, NC: University of North Carolina, FPG Child Development Institute.

DLM early childhood express. (2011). Desoto, TX: McGraw-Hill.

Dodge, D. T., Colker, L., & Heroman, C. (2010). *The creative curriculum for preschool* (5th ed.). Washington, DC: Teaching Strategies.

Domitrovich, C., Greenberg, M., Kusche, C., & Cortes, R. (2004). *PATHS preschool program (Promoting alternative thinking strategies)*. South Deerfield, MA: Channing Bete.

Eagle, J. W., Dowd-Eagle, S. E., & Sheridan, S. M. (2008). Best practices in school–community partnerships. In A. Thomas & J. Grimes (Eds.), *Best practices in school psychology* (Vol. 5, pp. 953–967). Bethesda, MD: National Association of School Psychologists.

Early Childhood Research Institute on Measuring Growth and Development. (1998–2000). *Individual growth and development indicators for preschool children: Picture naming/ expressing meaning, rhyming/early literacy, alliteration/early literacy, picture naming in Spanish/expressive meaning*. Minneapolis: University of Minnesota, Center for Early Education and Development.

Egger, H. L., & Angold, A. (2006). Common emotional and behavioral disorders in preschool children: Presentation, nosology, and epidemiology. *Journal of Child Psychology and Psychiatry, 47,* 313–337.

Elliott, S. N., & Gresham, F. M. (2007). *Social skills improvement system (SSIS) classwide intervention program teacher's guide*. Minneapolis, MN: Pearson.

Elliott, S. N., & Gresham, F. M. (2008). *Social skills improvement system (SSIS) intervention guide*. Minneapolis, MN: Pearson.Estrem, T. L. (2011). Expressive vocabulary development of immigrant preschoolers who speak Somali, Spanish, and Hmong. *Teaching English as a Second or Foreign Language: The Electronic Journal for English as a Second Language, 15*(1), 1–19.

Estrem, T. L., & McConnell, S. R. (2008). *Monitoring emergent literacy development of immigrant preschoolers who speak Somali, Spanish, or Hmong* (Technical Report #9). Minneapolis, MN: Center for Early Education and Development, University of Minnesota.

Fantuzzo, J., McWayne, C., Perry, M. A., & Childs, S. (2004). Multiple dimensions of family involvement and their relations to behavioral and learning competencies for urban, low-income children. *School Psychology Review, 33,* 467–480.

Feeney-Kettler, K. A. (2008). *Early identification of preschool students at risk for emotional and behavioral disorders: Development and validation of a parent–teacher screener* (Doctoral dissertation). University of Wisconsin-Madison.

Feeney-Kettler, K. A., Kratochwill, T. R., Kaiser, A. P., Hemmeter, M. L., & Kettler, R. J. (2010). Screening young children's risk for mental health problems: A review of four measures. *Assessment for Effective Intervention, 35,* 218–230.

Feeney-Kettler, K. A., Kratochwill, T. R., & Kettler, R. J. (20119). *Preschool behavior screening system*. Unpublished instrument, Vanderbilt University.

Feeney-Kettler, K. A., Kratochwill, T. R., & Kettler, R. J. (2012). Identification of preschool children at risk for emotional and behavioral disorders: Development and validation of a universal screening system. *Journal of School Psychology, 49,* 197–216.

Feil, E. G., Severson, H. H., & Walker, H. M. (1998). Screening for emotional and behavioral delays: The early screening project. *Journal of Early Intervention, 21,* 252–266.

Floyd, R. G., Hojnoski, R., & Key, J. (2006). Preliminary evidence of the technical adequacy of the preschool numeracy indicators. *School Psychology Review, 35*(4), 627–644.

Fox, L. Carta, J., Strain, P. S., Dunlap, G., & Hemmeter, M. L. (2010). Response to intervention and the Pyramid Model. *Infants & Young Children, 23*(1), 3–13.

Frank Porter Graham (FPG) Child Development Institute. (2012). *Recognition and response: RTI for pre-K*. Retrieved from http://www.randr.fpg.unc.edu/.

Fuchs, L. S., & Deno, S. L. (1991). Paradigmatic distinctions between instructionally relevant measurement models. *Exceptional Children, 57,* 488–499.

Gillis, M., West, T., & Coleman, M. R. (2010a). *Early learning observation and rating scale: Teacher's guide*. New York: National Center for Learning Disabilities.

Gillis, M., West, T., & Coleman, M. R. (2010b). *Early learning observation and rating scale: Development manual.* New York: National Center for Learning Disabilities.

Glover, T. A., & Albers, C. A. (2007). Considerations for evaluating universal screening instruments. *Journal of School Psychology, 45,* 117–135.

Goldstein, H., & Kaminski, R. (2010). *Research conducted by CRTIEC on Tier 2 and Tier 3 interventions.* Kansas City, KS: Center for Response to Intervention in Early Childhood, University of Kansas. Retrieved from http://www.crtiec.org/rti_summit/2010/19-goldstein-kaminski.shtml

Greenwood, C. R., Bradfield, T., Kaminiski, R., Linas, M., Carta, J. J., & Nylander, D. (2011). The Response to Intervention (RTI) approach in early childhood. *Focus on Exceptional Children, 43*(9), 1–22.

Gresham, F. M., & Elliott, S. N. (2008). *Social skills improvement system—Rating scales manual.* Minneapolis, MN: Pearson Assessments.

Halgunseth, L. C., Peterson, A., Stark, D. R., & Moodie, S. (2009). *Family engagement, diverse families, and early childhood education programs: An integrated review of the literature.* Washington, DC: National Association for the Education of Young Children. Retrieved from http://www.naeyc.org/files/naeyc/file/research/FamEngage.pdf

Heckman, J. H. (2000). *Invest in the very young.* Chicago, IL: Ounce of Prevention and the University of Chicago Harris School of Public Policy Studies. Retrieved from www.ounceofprevention.org/news/pdfs/HeckmanInvestInVeryYoung.pdf

Hemmeter, M. L., Ostrosky, M., & Fox, L. (2006). Social and emotional foundations for early learning: A conceptual model for intervention. *School Psychology Review, 35,* 583–601.

Hochstedt, K. S., Lei, P. W., DiPerna, J. C., & Morgan, P. L. (2011). Examining the dimensionality of EARLI literacy skill scores using nonlinear factor analysis. *Journal of Psychoeducational Assessment, 29*(5), 395–406.

Hojnoski, R. L., & Missall, K. N. (2010). Social development in preschool classrooms: Promoting engagement, competence, and school readiness. In M. R. Shinn & H. M. Walker (Eds.), *Interventions for achievement and behavior problems in a three-tier model including RTI* (pp. 703–728). Bethesda, MD: National Association of School Psychologists.

Hojnoski, R. L., Silberglitt, B., & Floyd, R. G. (2009). Numeracy indicators with a sample of preschoolers in Head Start. *School Psychology Review, 38*(3), 402–418.

Individuals with Disabilities Education Improvement Act (IDEA). (2004). P. L. 108-446 (20 U.S.C. 1400 et seq.).

Institute of Education Sciences. (2012). *What Works Clearinghouse.* Retrieved from http://ies.ed.gov/ncee/wwc/.

Jackson, R., McCoy, A., Pistorino, C., Wilkinson, A., Burghardt, J., Clark, M., Ross, C., … Swank, P. (2007). *National evaluation of Early Reading First: Final report.* Washington, DC: U.S. Government Printing Office.

Jimerson, S., Egeland, B., & Teo, A. (1999). A longitudinal study of achievement trajectories: Factors associated with change. *Journal of Educational Psychology, 91,* 116–126.

Kamphaus, R. W., & Reynolds, C. R. (2007). *BASC-2 behavioral and emotional screening system.* Minneapolis, MN: Pearson.

Kansas MTSS. (2008). *Kansas multi-tier system of supports.* Retrieved from http://www.kansasmtss.org/

Kansas State Department of Education. (2010). *The integration of MTSS and RTI.* Retrieved from http://www.kansasmtss.org/resources.htm

Kenny, H., Oliver, L., & Poppe, J. (2002). *Mental health services for children: An overview.* Retrieved from http://www.ncsl.org/programs/cyf/CPI.pdf

Kettler, R. J., & Feeney-Kettler, K. A. (2011). Screening systems and decision-making at the preschool level: Application of a comprehensive validity framework. *Psychology in the Schools, 48*(5), 430–441.

Klein, A., Starkey, P., & Ramirez, A. B. (2002). *Pre-K mathematics curriculum.* Glenview, IL: Scott Foresman.

Knopf, H. T., & Swick, K. J. (2008). Using our understanding of families to strengthen family involvement. *Early Childhood Education Journal, 35*, 419–427.

Lei, P., Wu, Q., DiPerna, J. C., & Morgan, P. L. (2009). Developing short forms of the EARLI numeracy measures: Comparison of item selection methods. *Educational and Psychological Measurement, 69*(5), 825–842.

Levitt, J. M., Saka, N., Hunter Romanelli, L., & Hoagwood, K. (2007). Early identification of mental health problems in schools: The status of instrumentation. *Journal of School Psychology, 45*, 163–191.

Linas, M. W., Carta, J. J., & Greenwood, C. R. (2010, June). *Taking a snapshot of early childhood response to intervention across the United States: 2009 and 2010.* Washington, DC: Head Start Research Conference.

Linas, M. W. Greenwood, C. R., & Carta, J. J. (2009, June). *Taking a snapshot of early childhood response to intervention across the states.* Paper presented at the Fourth Annual IES Research Conference, Washington, DC.

Literacy Partnership. (2007). *Partnering for literacy: A multi-disciplinary program for emergent and early reading success.* Retrieved from http://literacypartnershiperfgrant.com/

Maschinot, B. (2008). *The changing face of the United States: The influence of culture on child development.* Washington, DC: Zero to Three.

McGivern, J. E., Ray-Subramanian, C. E., & Auster, E. R. (2008). Best practices in establishing effective helping relationships. In A. Thomas & J. Grimes (Eds.), *Best practices in school psychology* (Vol. 5, pp. 1613–1632). Bethesda, MD: National Association of School Psychologists.

McWayne, C., Campos, R., & Owsianik, M. (2008). A multidimensional, multilevel examination of mother and father involvement among culturally diverse Head Start families. *Journal of School Psychology, 46*, 551–573.

Meisels, S. J., Marsden, D. B., Wiske, M. S., & Henderson, L. W. (1997). *Early screening inventory—Revised.* Ann Arbor, MI: Rebus.

Merrell, K. W. (2003). *Preschool and kindergarten behavior scales* (2nd ed.). Austin, TX: Pro-Ed.

Missall, K., & McConnell, S. (2004). *Psychometric characteristics of individual growth and development indicators: Picture naming, rhyming, and alliteration* (Technical report No. 8). Minneapolis, MN: Center for Early Education and Development, University of Minnesota.

National Association for the Education of Young Children (NAEYC) and National Council of Teachers of Mathematics. (2002). *Joint position statement on math. Early childhood mathematics: Promoting good beginnings.* Retrieved from http://naeyc.org/about/positions/psmath.asp

National Association for the Education of Young Children (NAEYC). (2009a). *Developmentally appropriate practice in early childhood programs serving children from birth through age 8.* Washington: DC. Author.

National Association for the Education of Young Children (NAEYC). (2009b). *Where we stand: On responding to linguistic and cultural diversity.* Washington: DC. Author.

National Association for the Education of Young Children, Division of Early Childhood of the Council for Exceptional Children, & National Headstart Association. (2012).

Frameworks for response to intervention in early childhood education: Description and implications (Draft). Retrieved September 23, 2012, from http://www.naeyc.org/content/frameworks-for-rti-in-ece

National Association of School Psychologists. (2003). *Early intervention services* (Position Statement). Bethesda, MD: Author.

National Association of School Psychologists. (2009). *Early childhood assessment* (Position Statement). Bethesda, MD: Author.

National Center for Education Research. (2008). *Effects of preschool curriculum programs on school readiness: Report from the Preschool Curriculum Evaluation Research initiative.* Retrieved from http://ies.ed.gov/ncer/pubs/20082009/index.asp

National Center for Learning Disabilities. (2009). *Roadmap to pre-K RTI: Applying response to intervention in preschool settings.* Retrieved from http://www.RTINetwork.org/PreKRTIRoadmap

National Professional Development Center on Inclusion. (2012). *Response to intervention (RTI) in early childhood: Building consensus on the defining features.* Chapel Hill, NC: The University of North Carolina, FPG Child Development Institute.

National Research Council. (2001). *Educating children with autism.* Washington, DC: National Academy Press.

National Research Council & Institute of Medicine. (2000). *From neurons to neighborhoods: The science of early childhood development.* Washington, DC: National Academy Press.

National Scientific Council on the Developing Child. (2008). *Mental health problems in early childhood can impair learning and behavior for life* (Working paper No. 6). Retrieved from http://www.developingchild.net

No Child Left Behind Act (NCLB). (2001). P.L. 107-110.

O'Connor, E. P., & Freeman, E. W. (2012). District-level considerations in supporting and sustaining RTI implementation. *Psychology in the Schools, 49*(3), 297–310. doi:10.1002/pits.21598

Office of Head Start, Administration for Children and Families, U.S. Department of Health and Human Services (2011). *The Head Start parent, family, and community engagement framework: Promoting family engagement and school readiness, from prenatal to age 8.* Arlington, VA: Head Start Resource Center.

Ortiz, A. A., & Yates, J. R. (2002). Considerations in the assessment of English language learners referred to special education. In A. Artiles & A. Ortiz (Eds.), *English language learners with special education needs: Identification, assessment, and instruction* (pp. 65–86). Washington, DC: Center for Applied Linguistics and Delta Systems.

Parlakian, R., & Lerner, C. (2008). *Your child's development: 24 to 30 months.* Washington, DC: Zero to Three. Retrieved from http://www.zerotothree.org/child-development/early-development/24-30handout.pdf

Patrick, K., Spear, B., Holt, K., & Sofka, D. (Eds.). (2001). *Bright futures in practice: Physical activity.* Arlington, VA: National Center for Education in Maternal and Child Health.

PBIS.org. (2012). *OSEP technical assistance center on effective schoolwide interventions: Positive behavioral interventions and supports.* Retrieved from www.pbis.org

Polignano, J. C., & Hojnoski, R. L. (2012). Preliminary evidence of the technical adequacy of additional curriculum-based measures for preschool mathematics. *Assessment for Effective Intervention, 37*(2), 70–83.

Powell, D., Dunlap, G., & Fox, L. (2006). Prevention and intervention for the challenging behaviors of toddlers and preschoolers. *Infants & Young Children: An Interdisciplinary Journal of Special Care Practices, 19*(1), 25–35.

Prior, J., & Gerard, M. R. (2007). *Family involvement in early childhood education: Research into practice.* Clifton Park, NY: Thomson Delmar Learning.

Reid, E. E., Morgan, P. L., DiPerna, J. C., & Lei, P. W. (2006). Development of measures to assess young children's early academic skills: Preliminary findings from a Head Start–university partnership. *Insights on Learning Disabilities, 3*(2), 25–38.

Reid, M. A., DiPerna, J. C., Morgan, P. L., & Lei, P. W. (2009). Reliability and validity evidence for the EARLI literacy probes. *Psychology in the Schools, 46*(10), 1023–1035.

Reynolds, C. R., & Kamphaus, R. W. (2004). *Behavior assessment system for children* (2nd ed.). Circle Pines, MN: American Guidance Service.

Reynolds, C. R., & Kamphaus, R. W. (2009). *BASC-2 progress monitor manual.* Minneapolis, MN: Pearson.

Rosenberg, S. A., Zhang, D., & Robinson, C. C. (2008). Prevalence of developmental delays and participation in early intervention services for young children. *Pediatrics, 121,* 1503–1509.

Roseth, C. J., Missall, K. N., & McConnell, S. R. (2012). Early literacy individual growth and development indicators (EL-IGDIs): Growth trajectories using a large, internet-based sample. *Journal of School Psychology, 50*(4), 483–501.

Russell, J., McCoy, A., Pistorino, C., Wilkinson, A., Burghardt, J., Clark, M., … Swank, P. (2007). *National evaluation of Early Reading First: Final report.* U.S. Department of Education, Institute of Education Sciences. Washington, DC: US Government Printing Office. Retrieved from http://ies.ed.gov/ncee/pdf/20074007.pdf

Ryan, J. B., Hughes, E. M., Katsiyannis, A., McDaniel, M., & Sprinkle, C. (2011). Research-based educational practices for students with autism spectrum disorders. *TEACHING Exceptional Children, 43*(3), 56–64.

Sailor, W., Dunlap, G., Sugai, G., & Horner, R. (Eds.). (2009). *Handbook of positive behavior support.* Boston, MA: Springer.

Sandall, S. R., & Schwartz, I. S. (2008). *Building blocks for teaching preschoolers with special needs* (2nd ed.). Baltimore, MD: Brookes.

Sattler, J. M. (2008). *Assessment of children: Cognitive applications* (5th ed.). La Mesa, CA: Author.

Shapiro, E. S. (2000). School psychology from an instructional perspective: Solving big, not little problems. *School Psychology Review, 29*(4), 560–572.

Sheridan, S. M., Clarke, B. L., Knoche, L. L. & Edwards, C. P. (2006). Effects of conjoint behavioral consultation in early childhood settings. *Early Education and Development, 17,* 593–617.

Sheridan, S. M., Knoche, L. L., Edwards, C. P., Bovaird, J. A., & Kupzyk, K. A. (2010). Parent engagement and school readiness: Effects of the getting ready intervention on preschool children's social-emotional competencies. *Early Education & Development, 21,* 125–156.

Sheridan, S. M., Knoche, L. L., Kupzyk, K. A., Edwards, C. P., & Marvin, C. A. (2011). A randomized trial examining the effects of parent engagement on early language and literacy: The getting ready intervention. *Journal of School Psychology, 49,* 361–383.

Sheridan, S. M., & Kratochwill, T. R. (2010). *Conjoint-behavioral consultation: Promoting family-school connections and interventions* (2nd ed.). New York: Springer.

Sices, L., Egbert, L., & Mercer, M. B. (2009). Sugar-coaters and straight talkers: Communicating about developmental delays in primary care. *Pediatrics, 124,* e705–e713.

Squires, J. Bricker, D., & Twombly, E. (2002). *Ages and stages questionnaires: Social and emotional.* Baltimore, MD: Brookes.

Strein, W., Hoagwood, K., & Cohn, A. (2003). School psychology: A public health perspective I. Prevention, populations, and systems change. *Journal of School Psychology, 41,* 23–38.

Stevenson, H. W., & Newman, R. S. (1986). Long-term predictions of achievement and attitudes in mathematics and reading. *Child Development, 57,* 646–659.

Teaching Strategies. (2010a). *Teaching strategies GOLD assessment system.* Bethesda, MD: Author.

Teaching Strategies. (2010b). *Research foundation: The creative curriculum.* Bethesda, MD: Author.

U.S. Bureau of the Census. (2010). Estimated resident population ages 3 through 5, by state: 2001, 2009, and 2010. Retrieved from http://www.ideadata.org/PopulationData.asp

U.S. Department of Commerce. (2010). Percentage of the population 3 to 34 years old enrolled in school, by age group: Selected years, 1940 through 2009. Retrieved from http://nces.ed.gov/programs/digest/d10/tables/dt10_007.asp

U.S. Department of Education. (2010). Children with disabilities receiving special education under part B of the Individuals with Disabilities Education Act. Retrieved from http://www.ideadata.org/PopulationData.asp

U.S. Department of Health and Human Services (USDHHS). (1999). *Mental health: A report of the Surgeon General.* Rockville, MD: United States Department of Health and Human Services, Substance Abuse and Mental Health Administration, Center for Mental Health Services, National Institutes of Health, National Institute of Mental Health.

VanDerHeyden, A. M., Broussard, C., & Cooley, A. (2006). Further development of measures of early math performance for preschoolers. *Journal of School Psychology, 44,* 533–553.

VanDerHeyden, A. M., Broussard, C., Fabre, M., Stanley, J., Legendre, J., & Creppell, R. (2004). Development and validation of curriculum-based measures of math performance for preschool children. *Journal of Early Intervention, 27*(1), 27–41.

Vig, S., & Sanders, M. (2007). Assessment of mental retardation. In M. R. Brassard & A. E. Boehm, *Preschool assessment: Principles and practices* (pp. 420–446). New York: Guilford.

Walker, H. M., Severson, H. H., & Feil, E. G. (1995). *Early screening project: User manual.* Longmont, CO: Sopris West.

Weiss, H., Caspe, M., & Lopez, M. E. (2006). *Family involvement in early childhood education.* Cambridge, MA: Harvard Family Research Project, Harvard Graduate School of Education. Retrieved from http://www.hfrp.org/family-involvement/publications-resources/family-involvement-in-early-childhood-education

Weiss, H. B., Bouffard, S. M., Bridglall, B. L., & Gordon, E. W. (2009). *Reframing family involvement in education: Supporting families to support educational equity.* New York: The Campaign for Educational Equity, Teachers College, Columbia University. Retrieved from http://www.equitycampaign.org/i/a/document/12018_EquityMatters-Vol5_Web.pdf

Whitehurst, G. J., & Lonigan, C. J. (1998). Child development and emergent literacy. *Child Development, 69,* 848–872.

Wireless Generation. (2010). *mCLASS CIRCLE: User guide.* Brooklyn, NY: Author.

World Health Organization. (2012). *Mental health.* Retrieved from http://www.who.int/mental_health/en/.

Young, R. M., Snow, L. M., Frech, C., & Shields, L. (2011). *Developing socially competent and emotionally resilient young children through an early childhood RtI framework.* Retrieved from http://www.rtinetwork.org/learn/rti-in-pre-kindergarten/developing-socially-competent-and-emotionally-resilient-young-children

Zhang, C., & Bennett, T. (2003). Facilitating the meaningful participation of culturally and linguistically diverse families in the IFSP and IEP process. *Focus on Autism and Other Developmental Disabilities, 18,* 51–59.

Index

academic interventions: overview, 33–34, 44; Creative Curriculum System for Preschool, 36–37; DLM Early Childhood Express, 37; and evidence-based curricula, 40–42; and the Literacy Partnership, 42–43; Prairie Children Preschool, 43–44; Recognition and Response (R&R) program, 43; state initiatives, 44; Tier 1, 34–37; Tier 2, 5, 37–39; Tier 3, 36, 39

Ages and Stages Questionnaires: Social-Emotional (ASQ-SE), 53, 54, *55*

Alphabet Recitation, 27–28

American Psychological Association (APA), 17–18

BASC-2 Progress Monitor instruments, 70

Behavior and Emotional Screening Program (BASC-2 BESS), 53, 54, *55*

behavior incident reports (BIRs), 68

behavioral functioning. *See* social-emotional and behavioral functioning screening

Building Blocks model, 64–65

Center for Early Education Development (CEED), 25–26

Center for Improving the Readiness of Children for Learning and Education (CIRCLE), 26–27

Center for Response to Intervention in Early Childhood (CRTIEC), 6–7, 25, 37–38, 39

Children's Learning Institute (CLI), 26–27

CIRCLE Phonological Awareness, Language, and Literacy System plus (C-PALLS+), 26

cognitive milestones, 77–78

collaborative problem solving, 3

communication milestones, 76–77

conjoint/collaborative behavioral consultation (CBC), 99–103

Council for Exceptional Children (CEC), 15–17

Creative Curriculum System for Preschool, 36–37, 44

criterion-referenced tests (CRTs), 24

curriculum-based assessment (CBA), 24

curriculum-based measurements (CBMs), 21–22, 24

developmental disability identification: overview, 75–76, 90; Anthony case example, 88–89; and cognitive milestones, 77–78; and communication milestones, 76–77; and cultural and linguistic diversity, 84–85; developmental assessment purpose, 83–84; discussing developmental concerns with parents of guardians, 81–82; and early childhood inclusion, 85–88; and informed interventions, 85; Mia case example, 89–90; motor and self-care milestones, 78–80; and multiple assessment methods, 84; and parental discussions with health care providers, 82; and referrals for early childhood special education, 83; and referrals for early intervention, 82–83; and social milestones, 80–81

developmental screening, preschool, 22–23

diversity: and developmental disability identification, 84–85; and screening tool selection, 52; working with culturally and linguistically diverse children and families, *16*

DLM Early Childhood Express, 37

early academic skills screening, 20–32; overview, 20–22, 32; and curriculum-based measurements (CBMs), 21–22, 24; and early literacy skills, 24–28, 37–38; and early math skills, 29–31, 38–39; and general outcome measures (GOMs), 21; preschool developmental screening, 22–23; preschool instructional screening, 23–24; and Sherman Academy, 20, 23–24, 32

Early Arithmetic, Reading, and Learning Indicators (EARLI), 27–28, 31

early childhood inclusion, 85–88

early childhood programming. *See* multitiered systems of supports (MTSS)

early intervention services, 18

Early Learning Observation and Rating Scale (ELORS), 28, 31, 71–72

early literacy skills, 24–28, 37–38

early math skills, 29–31, 38–39

Early Reading First program, 12

Early Screening Inventory–Revised, 23

Early Screening Project (ESP), 53–54, 55

ethics, standards for educational and psychological testing, 14

Even Start program, 12–13

evidence-based curricula, 40–42

evidence-based practices, 3, 15–16

Expressive Vocabulary, 27–28

family engagement: overview, 91–92, 104; addressing barriers to family–school partnerships, 98–99; conjoint/collaborative behavioral consultation (CBC), 99–103; and MTSS, 3; promotion of, 94–98; research on, 92–94

general education, 5

general outcome measures (GOMs), 21, 26, 27, 29, 30

Glenview Early Childhood Program, 73

implementation fidelity, 3

Individual Education Program (IEP), 11

individual growth and development indicators (IGDIs): and CRTIEC, 7; and

the Literacy Partnership, 43; and Tier 2 supports, 35

Individuals with Disabilities Education Improvement Act (IDEA), 1–2, 10–12, 23

informed interventions, 85

infrastructure for screening implementation, 49–50

instructional screening, preschool, 23–24

interventions, informed, 85. *See also* academic interventions; social-emotional and behavioral interventions

law, ethical standards, and guidelines for MTSS: overview, 10, 19; American Psychological Association (APA), 17–18; Council for Exceptional Children (CEC), 15–17; and IDEA, 1–2, 10–12; National Association for the Education of Young Children (NAEYC), 15, *16*; National Association of School Psychologists (NASP), 18–19; National Professional Development Center on Inclusion (NPDCI), 17; and NCLB, 12–13; and Race to the Top–Early Learning Challenge (RTT–ELC), 13–14; standards for educational and psychological testing, 14

Letter Naming, 27–28

Letter Sounds, 27–28

the Literacy Partnership, 6, 42–43

mCLASS+, 26–27, 29, 71

motor and self-care milestones, 78–80

multitiered systems of supports (MTSS): overview, 1–2, 8–9; Center for Response to Intervention in Early Childhood (CRTIEC), 6–7; Colorado State Department of Education, 8; core principles of, 2; and early childhood programming, 1–3; future of, 108–10; implementation considerations, 105–8, *107*; and integration of screening, 57–58; and the Literacy Partnership, 6; and pyramid model, 7; Recognition and Response (R&R) program, 6; responsibility for, 5; Rockford Early

Childhood Program, 7–8; Tier 1, 2, and 3 services, 3–5, *4*

National Association for the Education of Young Children (NAEYC), 15, *16*
National Association of School Psychologists (NASP), 18–19
National Center on Response to Intervention, 21
National Professional Development Center on Inclusion (NPDCI), 17
No Child Left Behind (NCLB), 12–13
normative population, 52

office discipline referrals (ODRs), 68–69

Parent–Individual Child ELORS form, 28
parental and family engagement. *See* family engagement
Pattern Completion PNI, 30–31
Positive Behavioral Interventions and Supports (PBIS), 62–63
Prairie Children Preschool, 43–44, 73–74
Pre-K Mathematics, 39
Pre-Kindergarten Early Numeracy Screener, 29–30
Preschool Behavior Screening System (PBSS), 53, 54, *55*, 58–59
preschool developmental screening, 22–23
Preschool Evaluation Curriculum Research (PECR), 40–41
Preschool Individual Growth and Development Indicators (Preschool IGDIs), 25–26
preschool instructional screening, 23–24
Preschool Numeracy Indicators (PNIs), 30–31
progress monitoring in young children, 68–69
Promoting Alternative Thinking Strategies (PATHS), 66
Promoting Awareness in Speech Sounds (PASS), 42
psychometric properties and screening tool selection, 50–52
Public Law 94-142 and 99-457, 11
Pyramid Model, 7, 63–64

Race to the Top–Early Learning Challenge (RTT–ELC), 13–14
Receptive and Expressive Approach to Language and Learning (REALL), 42
Recognition and Response (R&R) program, 6, 43
Response to Intervention (RTI), 21, 28
Rockford Early Childhood Program, 7–8, 72–73

School-Wide Positive Behavioral Interventions and Supports (SWPBIS), 62–63
screening tools: and children from culturally and linguistically diverse backgrounds, 52; evaluation of, 50; examples of, 53–56, *55*; implementation infrastructure, 49–50; and knowledge of psychometric properties, 50–52; and MTSS, 2–3; selection of, 47–52. *See also* early academic skills screening; socio-emotional and behavioral functioning screening
Section 5542 of NCLB, 13
Segmenting, 27
Sherman Academy, 20, 23–24, 32, 33, 58–59, 61, 72
skill-focused listening centers (SFLCs), 38
social-emotional and behavioral functioning screening: overview, 45–46, 59–60; and early childhood populations, 56–57; integration into MTSS, 57–58; need for, 46–47; reasons for screening, 46–47; screening tool examples, 53–56, *55*; screening tool selection, 47–52; Sherman Academy case example, 58–59; when to screen, 56
social-emotional and behavioral interventions: overview, 61–62, 74; BASC-2 Progress Monitor instruments, 70; Building Blocks model, 64–65; Early Learning Observation and Rating Scale (ELORS), 71–72; Glenview Early Childhood Program, 73; mCLASS+ system, 71; Prairie Children Preschool, 73–74; progress monitoring in young children, 68–69; Promoting Alternative

social-emotional and behavioral
interventions (*continued*): Thinking
Strategies (PATHS), 66; and the
Pyramid Model, 63–64; Rockford Early
Childhood Program, 72–73; School-
Wide Positive Behavioral Interventions
and Supports (SWPBIS), 62–63; Social
Skills Improvement System Rating
Scales (SSIS-RS), 69–70; Social Skills
Improvement System (SSIS) Classwide
Intervention Program, 65–66; Social
Skills Improvement System (SSIS)
Intervention Guide, 66–67; Teaching
Strategies GOLD Assessment System,
70–71; Tier 1 interventions, 65–66;
Tier 2 interventions, 66–67; Tier 3
interventions, 67–68
social milestones, 80–81
Social Skills Improvement System Rating
Scales (SSIS-RS), 69–70

Social Skills Improvement System (SSIS)
Classwide Intervention Program, 65–66
Social Skills Improvement System (SSIS)
Intervention Guide, 66–67
Sound Deletion, 27
special education, 5, 83
standards for educational and psychological
testing, 14, 18–19
System to Enhance Educational Performance
(STEEP), 30

Teacher–Individual Child ELORS form, 28
Teaching Strategies GOLD Assessment
System, 70–71
testing standards, 14
Tier 1, 2, and 3 services: and multitiered
systems of supports (MTSS), 3–5, 4. *See
also* academic interventions and progress
monitoring

Whole Class ELORS form, 28